Mother Shock

Mother Shock

Loving Every (Other) Minute of It

Andrea J. Buchanan

**SEAL
PRESS**

MOTHER SHOCK: Loving Every (Other) Minute of It

© 2003 by Andrea J. Buchanan

Published by Seal Press
An Imprint of Avalon Publishing Group Incorporated
161 William St., 16th Floor
New York, NY 10038

Library of Congress Cataloging-in-Publication Data is available.

ISBN 1-58005-082-4

9 8 7 6 5 4 3 2

Designed by Paul Paddock

Printed in the United States of America
Distributed by Publishers Group West

To Emi, who broke me in, and Nate,
who will hopefully reap the benefits

Contents

Introduction

Imagine you have just moved to a foreign country. You have the worst case of jet lag ever. The guidebook you brought, which seemed so comprehensive before you left home, does not tell you everything you need to know. You do not yet speak the language, and everything is confusing. Your spouse or traveling companion either hasn't come with you or gets to go back home each morning, coming to visit you only at the end of the day. In this new place, the customs are very different. Your natural ways of behaving and interacting are no longer appropriate. Despite the newness of everything, in this particular country you are expected to adapt immediately. But the rhythms of life are different here, and you are constantly sleep-deprived. You miss your old life, where everything was familiar. You miss your friends back home, who only imagine the excitement of your travels and are unable to fully understand the difficulties you describe.

This is what it feels like for many of us when we become mothers: we find we have entered into a strange new world with a language, culture, time zone, and set of customs all its own. Until we become acclimated to this new, seemingly unfathomable territory, we exist in a state of culture shock. We are in mother shock.

When I became pregnant, I scoured the Web for information. I read about women trying to have babies; women who battled infertility; women who were three months pregnant, six months pregnant, nine months pregnant; women who miscarried early; women who delivered late; women who loved being pregnant; women who hated it. I tested the Chinese Conception Calendar to predict my baby's gender; I looked through the endless selections of baby names; I comparison-shopped for strollers. I signed up for e-mail newsletters detailing the rapid, invisible development of my in-utero guest. I posted on discussion boards and argued over parenting techniques with other women who were not yet mothers. I learned about Toni Weschler's *Taking Charge of Your Fertility*, Ferberizing, and the horrors of Ezzo and Bucknam's *Baby Wise*. I discovered the bible that is Fields's *Baby Bargains*. I enrolled in birthing class and began to watch the cable series *A Baby Story*. In short, I tried to do all the research I could and know everything there was to know about my biggest project to date: having a baby.

But then I had my baby. Suddenly I was in unfamiliar territory. I'd had nine months to anticipate being a mother, and then about thirty seconds to snap into being one. When I eventually left the hospital, shell-shocked by the whirlwind of sleep-deprivation, two days of pre-labor, an excruciatingly epidural-free delivery, and the unbelievable reality of my baby in my arms instead of snugly lodged inside me, all I could think was: why does no one talk about this?

It wasn't just that the sun seemed so bright to me after being inside for two days, or that the cars driving past suddenly appeared to be death traps on wheels, or that the streets were full of grime and dirt I hadn't noticed before, or even that I saw the people around us as the germ-delivery systems they really were. It was that everything was fragile, everything was tenuous: I had crossed over to a strange new world, a world where another person's life literally depended on me, and everything seemed at the same time both more real and more unreal. I realized I had spent the past nine months learning how to be pregnant, not how to be a mother —and being pregnant was the part that came naturally. Finally, after all my wondering, after all my preparation, after all my research, I had crossed over to the other side, and instead of being happy, I was in shock. Why had no one told me about this? Why had people been talking about slings and bouncy seats instead of telling me what motherhood is really like? Why had I never bothered to ask?

I had packed my bag for the hospital, but I ended up going on a much longer trip. I felt that in becoming a mother I had been transported to a foreign country with a whole new language, a different culture, a striking political landscape, and a punishing time zone to adjust to—and this sense of being in a strange land was all the more jarring since, of course, I hadn't left home.

Suddenly I was allowed only a few nonconsecutive hours of sleep a night, yet I still needed to function normally to care for a tiny, incredibly loud baby who didn't speak my language. Suddenly I had to know how to interpret my baby's cries, which in the beginning sounded merely like incessant screaming, not nuanced vocalizations full of clues as to what she needed. Suddenly I had to assume the mantle of responsibility for another human's life despite the fact that I barely felt responsible for my own. Suddenly I had to navigate my way through baby books, parenting articles, and advice from experts, grandparents, well-meaning friends, and complete strangers. Suddenly I had to be the one to know which was the safest, best, most baby-friendly stroller/car seat/highchair/sling/bassinet/baby food and where to find the cheapest/most environmentally friendly/least politically offensive place to buy it. Suddenly I was supposed to be the authority on all things related to my child. I was a new citizen in a brand-new country, and not only was I supposed to be immediately acclimated to living there, I was supposed to be the President.

But although it seemed that my entire world had shifted in the course of one exhausting, joyous, eventful day, it didn't seem as though anyone else had noticed. I waited for that mythical maternal instinct to kick in, waited for someone—a mother, my mother, any mother—to acknowledge that yes, really, everything does feel different and new and difficult, and that's okay. But nothing kicked in aside from sleep deprivation, fear, and self-doubt, and what I heard was that newborns are easy, that mothering, at the beginning at least, is not that hard. So I suffered my culture shock in silence, and as I began navigating my new surroundings with my daughter in the world instead of inside me, I silently wondered why I couldn't cope as easily with that transition as I had with changes in my pre-maternal life.

My sense of emotional dislocation reminded me of what I'd read about geographical dislocation: the phenomenon of culture shock and the general fish-out-of-water experience a person has when uprooted from her normal environment. So I did some research and discovered that the similarity between culture shock and what I was experiencing as a new mother was even more pronounced than I had imagined. The term "culture shock" was first coined nearly half a century ago by anthropologist Kalvero Oberg to describe the anxiety produced when a person moves to a completely new environment. In general, I learned, there are four phases to the adjustment cycle:

1. Initial euphoria, also referred to as the "honeymoon" stage, usually lasting from a few weeks to a month, where the newness of the experience is exciting rather than overwhelming;

2. Irritation/hostility, the "crisis" stage, in which many of the things the traveler initially found intriguing and exciting now seem annoying, frustrating, depressing, or overwhelming;

3. Recovery, where the traveler eventually becomes acclimated to the new country and feels less isolated; and

4. Adjustment, the final phase, in which the traveler can function in both cultures with confidence.

These phases of adjustment seemed to correspond so neatly with the first year of motherhood, I realized Oberg had provided a perfect description of the process I was in the midst of—this dislocation, this coming to grips with an entirely new way of living, was a kind of culture shock. It was mother shock.

A mother's culture shock, what I call "mother shock," is the transitioning period of the first year of new motherhood. It is the clash between expectation and result, theory and reality. It is the twilight zone of twenty-four-hour-a-day living, where life is no longer neatly divided into day and night, the triple-threat impact of hormonal imbalance, sleep deprivation, and physical exhaustion. It is the stress of trying to acclimate as quickly as possible to the immediacy of mothering, a new conception of oneself and one's role in the family and in the world, a new fearful level of responsibility, a new delegation of domestic duties, and a newly reduced amount of sleep.

Mother shock is not merely the hormonal plummet of the short-lasting "baby blues," and it is not the medical emergency that is acute postpartum depression. Mother shock is the transition, the period of adjustment to the weight of all the things required of mothers, a weight that presents itself all at once. (For that reason, I think of mother shock as something almost exclusively limited to first-time mothers. Mothers of two or more children certainly have their own overwhelming initial experiences, but that element of surprise shock is missing.)

Like the traditional breakdown of culture shock into four phases of adjustment, I conceived of mother shock as comprising a cycle of stages:

1. Mother Love (honeymoon stage, the first month): The pure joy of a mother's bonding with her newborn, analogous to the "honeymoon phase" of culture shock. This is the Hallmark-moment experience of maternal bliss that we routinely see in the media and expect to enjoy ourselves.

2. Mother Shock (crisis, months two to six): After a few weeks, the stress of the new situation—and in many cases the chronic lack of sleep—begins to take its toll. In culture shock, the second stage is mostly sparked by unmet expectations and

the strangeness of being cut off from cultural cues. The second stage of mother shock can also include those features, with the added critical factor of sleep deprivation. No matter what type of sleeper your baby is, chances are you're not getting the same amount of sleep your body has grown accustomed to for the last twenty- or thirty-odd years. A chronic sleep deficit can be brutal, and it can also strongly affect judgment, perspective, and sense of well-being. With little sleep and first-time-parent nerves, disillusionment, frustration, and self-doubt can begin to set in. In addition, new mothers are inundated with often conflicting advice from friends, family, doctors, and even complete strangers. This can undermine a new mother's confidence, especially if she is insecure about her parenting skills or is exhausted (as new mothers usually are). A new mother may feel overwhelmed by the immediacy of her baby's needs and may also feel isolated. A mother in this stage may feel conflicted about her postpartum body, about returning to work or not returning to work, about breast-feeding or being unable to breast-feed. She may experience depression, and it is in this stage that postpartum depression can set in for some women.

3. Mother Tongue (recovery, months seven to nine): Day by day, so gradually it might not even be noticeable at first, a mother becomes acclimated to the routine of life with an infant. Physically, her postpartum body may begin to resemble the one she had pre-pregnancy, and either her baby

has begun to sleep for longer stretches of time, or she is now used to getting by on interrupted and generally reduced sleep. By this point her baby is also becoming more interactive (e.g., smiling, cooing, laughing), and with more "proof" that everything is turning out fine, the mother can feel more confident in her parenting choices, less thrown by changes in routine, and generally more comfortable in her new role.

4. Mother Land (adjustment, months nine to twelve): This is the point at which a mother feels more or less fluent in mothering. She feels comfortable in her new role and has assimilated to this new place in her life. She is no longer a stranger in a strange land, and she may even find it difficult to imagine ever returning to the way things were before.

Not every stage of mother shock is discrete, and not every mother will experience each stage in the same order (or duration) in which I have described them. But nearly every new mother will experience some aspect of this total period of adjustment. I see mother shock as being twofold: the series of stages I have laid out, a timeline of adjusting to life as a mom; and the less temporally limited experience of motherhood in general. Mother love is something we can experience whether our babies are three weeks or three years old. Mother shock—our anger or disappointment or frustration as mothers—can be sparked from dealing with a colicky newborn or a tantruming toddler. Mother tongue, mastery of the intricacies of mothering, is something that we revisit sometimes monthly as our children change their routines or evolve developmentally. And mother land, the feeling of contentment at being a mother, is someplace we might reach with an infant sleeping on our shoulders or with a pre-schooler saying "I love you" for the very first time.

When I speak about mother shock with other mothers, many of them readily identify the feeling: the disconnect, the giddy joy of caring for a new life contrasted with the gnawing fear of falling short, the numbness that got them through the blurry, sleep-deprived days and nights of the first three months of their child's life. There is a light-bulb moment I can actually see happening when we talk about mother shock and put those difficult months of transition in context. Shock is generally not what comes to mind when picturing a new mother and her tiny infant, and yet when I compare the shock of new motherhood to the experience of culture shock, mothers get it. They recognize themselves in the description of a traveler in a strange land, they relate to the stress of trying to acclimate in the face of information overload. They are relieved to finally put a name to what we new mothers experience as we hover in the gap between our past world and our present, trying bravely to put aside our own needs to tend to those of our defenseless newborns, attempting to navigate the sheer strangeness of so much responsibility and so much selflessness on so little sleep.

• • •

This book is an exploration of mother shock from the inside out, featuring essays written during the first three years of my daughter's life. I have organized the essays by subject matter rather than in pure chronological progression, to loosely correspond to the stages of mother shock I have described. In the first section, "Mother Love," I write about not only the joy of being a mother but also my misconceptions about motherhood and my pre-partum worries about what it would be like. In "Mother Shock" I explore the darker feelings of maternal anger, frustration, and ambivalence. In the third section, "Mother Tongue," I write about learning to speak the language, scaling the learning curve of early motherhood, and my adventures in navigating everything from playgroup politics to learning the hard way why no one should ever take an eighteen-month-old to a business lunch. The final section, "Mother Land," features essays on what it's like to embrace motherhood, in all its complexity, reconciling my pre-maternal life with my current one and feeling comfortable walking around both with and without a stroller between me and the rest of the world.

When I first left the hospital with my baby, looking at the world for the first time as a mother, I asked myself, "Why does no one really talk about this?" As I grappled with my own experience of mother shock I realized why: it is problematic to discuss the difficulties of mothering without seeming ungrateful, uncaring, unappreciative, or unbalanced. It is difficult to contradict the conventional assumption that motherhood is noble and joyous and uncomplicated. But just because women have been having babies since there were babies to be had doesn't mean that becoming a mother isn't profoundly life-changing. Having a baby takes a matter of hours; becoming a mother is a much more gradual transition.

I

Mother Love

Honeymoon stage. An initial reaction of enchantment, fascination, enthusiasm, admiration and cordial, friendly, superficial relationships with hosts.

—Kalvero Oberg

Initial euphoria: Most people begin their new assignment with great
expectations and a positive mind-set. If anything, they come with expectations that are too high and attitudes that are too positive toward the
host country and toward their own prospective experiences in it.

—The University of Iowa's Web site on culture shock

My world shrunk to the size of her body. Immersed in her smell, her feed-
ings, her needs, I couldn't imagine doing anything without her, that didn't
involve her. . . . Totally absorbed, I lost myself within the tiny coil, the perfect comma, of her body.   —Nora Okja Keller

I looked at this tiny, perfect creature and it was as though a light switch
had been turned on. A giant rush of love flooded out of me.

—Madeleine L'Engle

Birth of a Mother: Part 1

My mother worked as a teacher while I was growing up, and over the years I eavesdropped on a number of juicy conversations about the woes of the profession. But by far the favorite topic of my mother and her female co-workers was the labor and delivery of their own children. Inevitably, as they met over a pitcher of vodka and orange juice to pound out progress reports or report cards or end-of-the-year evaluations, the conversation would turn from the students and parents they'd like to throttle to the horrific rite of passage each had experienced bringing her own kids into the world.

"Well, *this* one," my mom would say with a nod in my general direction (while I, of course, would be doing my best impersonation of someone reading a book and not listening), "*this* one had me in labor for hours—thirty-six hours of labor! Please! I'll take a root canal any day!"

"Tell me about it," someone else would chime in. "I pushed for ten hours before they gave up and did the C-section. Ten hours!" And they all would sigh in appreciation and reach for another round of drinks. Occasionally the tone would become more serious and all the teachers would lean their heads in, huddling around the table. Then it was all whispers, murmurs, the occasional scary-sounding word or phrase bubbling to the surface: "bleeding," "episiotomy," "postpartum depression."

These conversations seemed to last for hours, and though I heard many versions of the same stories year after year, I never tired of listening. It was mesmerizing in the perverse way that traffic accidents and horror movies are mesmerizing. I was drawn in to the drama as much as I was repelled by the frankness of their discussions, and I remember marveling that anyone could talk so much about anything that had happened so long ago. It was the kind of knowledge no one had ever shared with me face-to-face, and I had the sense that I was listening in on a secret, getting the inside scoop on something that might actually be personally relevant to me later on. It was thrilling and terrifying all at once.

"What are they all still doing here?" my sister would ask eventually, trying to see how long she could sneak in some forbidden TV while the teachers' bar was still open.

"They're all sitting around talking about giving birth," I'd reply, and we'd both roll our eyes.

"Gross."

That about summed up our burgeoning teenage attitudes toward the messy complications of the female body. At a time when our physical nature was a constant source of agony for us—all these unanticipated changes, all these hormones, these hips and breasts and zits—it was sickening, really, how they all kept talking about the bothersome things their bodies did. There they were, six ladies sitting around talking about private stuff, personal stuff, stuff that no one talks about. Didn't they realize when they said things like "pushing the baby out" that what they meant was that the baby was emerging from a vagina? Who needs to share that kind of detail with other people? Granted, it was fascinating that they all had this common experience to discuss. But it was still with a sense of foreboding that my sister and I listened, our rolling eyes and our smart remarks obscuring the emerging sense that our bodies had yet more in store for us—and that it wouldn't be pretty.

When I was in the seventh and eighth grades, my mother enrolled me in a Lutheran private school to evade school-district restrictions that would have mandated my certain torture at the hands of the junior-high kids at the local public school. Unfortunately, since I was almost a full two years younger and a foot shorter than most of my classmates, I was not spared any social humiliation. But I did learn a thing or two about the Old Testament.

The Bible class was pretty boring, but we spent a lot of time on Creation and the Garden of Eden, which made quite an impression on me. I learned that there was pain and suffering in the world because of one woman who wouldn't listen, and that as punishment, for the rest of eternity, men would have to work for a living and women would have to submit to their husbands and labor in pain to bring their sons and daughters into the world. Even though at the time I couldn't sort out the real problem with that scenario, my ears perked up when the teacher mentioned the bearing-children-in-pain part. It certainly did sound painful, according to what I'd already overheard.

I asked the teacher, "So, because Eve ate the apple, women have to have really painful childbirth?"

"Yes!" he said excitedly.

"So, before Eve ate the apple, it didn't hurt to have kids?" I pressed.

This presented a problem. Evidently, before Eve ate the apple, the teacher did his best to tentatively explain, Adam and Eve "didn't know" how to have kids. As the teacher's explanation progressed, there was a lot of tittering from the back of the room.

"So, if Eve hadn't eaten the apple, no one would know how to, you know, 'do it'?" asked one of the smart-mouthed eighth-grade boys.

"So it's a *good* thing that she ate the apple!" said another.

"Listen, the question was about women having to suffer in childbirth," said the flustered teacher, trying to evade the entire sex discussion. "And the answer is yes, childbirth is really painful. We don't know what the world might have been like if Eve hadn't eaten the apple, but she did, and now this is the lot all women have to bear. But here's the important thing," he said, and paused for dramatic effect. "You can ask any woman you know—you can ask your mom when you go home today"—a suggestion that evinced uncomfortable snickering from the class—"the fact is that it's very painful, but when it's over, the woman just completely forgets the pain. She can't remember it. She's so overjoyed to have brought a child into God's world, the pain is completely forgotten. Completely."

This quieted everyone down for a moment. How could something hurt so bad and be so painful and then be so quickly forgotten? From what I'd heard listening to my mother's teacher friends, it didn't sound like anyone had forgotten a thing.

The teacher continued. "Eve ate the apple, and as a consequence, men work and toil to support their families, and women have to endure the pain of childbirth. Both men and women suffer equally as a result of Eve's transgression."

"It doesn't sound so equal to me," I said to the teacher. "I think I'd rather go to work than have a baby."

When I first became pregnant, I craved not only spicy chicken sandwiches and fries but also information. I realized that one Bible class and a childhood of eavesdropping on my mom and her friends wasn't going to cut it in terms of preparing me for the reality of childbirth and parenthood.

So I got right to work, thumbing through books and surfing the Net for stories of labor, delivery, and beyond.

I bought the bible of pregnancy, *What to Expect When You're Expecting*, and realized that the health of my unborn child depended on my adhering to a strict diet that made liberal use of wheat germ and powdered milk. I also learned that I was already well on my way to creating problems for myself and my baby down the road since at eight weeks into pregnancy I'd already gained more than I was supposed to for the entire first trimester. The information I found online was more diverse, and much of it came from actual pregnant women and mothers. Still, a lot of what I read in the forums in which I lurked was just as frightening as the strict *What to Expect* doctrine: childbirth was an industry, doctors were negligent—they wanted women to labor flat on their backs, they encouraged C-sections so they could schedule their vacations—and the only way to safeguard against intervention was to have a midwife and birth at home in a Jacuzzi. Pregnancy and childbirth evidently was a time when a woman had to be hypervigilant against the routine misogyny of the medical profession if she had any hopes of avoiding forceps, vacuums, episiotomies, epidurals, C-sections, improper latching, or an otherwise overmedicalized experience of what should be the orgasmic completion of the union of a single sperm and egg.

I began to realize that these early kinds of choices—doctor or midwife, hospital or home birth, epidural or "natural"

—were already determining the kind of mother I would be: bottle or breast, cry-it-out or attachment parenting, day care or stay-at-home. It seemed like every decision along the way was fraught with the politics of a larger choice, and like a good student, I wanted to be sure to make the right one.

My husband and I signed up for a labor-and-delivery class, one of those once-a-week-for-one-month ones, and showed up for each class on time with notebooks. I listened as the instructor extolled the virtues of co-parenting, breast-feeding, and "natural" childbirth, careful to note that despite the fact that she was a hospital employee, she probably would have passed muster among the hard-core Internet birth junkies. We watched low-budget videos with questionable production values educating us about sudden infant death syndrome, the importance of breast-feeding, and how to breathe properly during labor. We watched a film following several couples as they went through labor and delivery, the women serenely rocking in comfortable-looking chairs, the men smoothing their part-ners' hair and offering ice chips when requested. There was no movie of women screaming in agony or suffering in unbelievable pain, despite the fact that the instructor informed us that giving birth is probably one of the most painful things you can experience and survive (at least in this century). It seemed that if you had a birth plan, a doula, ice chips, comfy seating, and a docile mate, the whole giving birth thing wasn't that bad. It was only if you were tense, had body issues, or were planning to formula-feed that childbirth would be really painful.

I had gathered a lot of information: from my eavesdropping as a kid I learned that bearing a child was something so momentous that women talked about it for years afterward, though evidently it wasn't all that horrible since they could laugh over it among friends. From junior high I learned that it hurt but that women deserve a little suffering, and that once it's over it's forgotten. From the books I learned that if you don't eat bagels or french fries and keep your weight down—and if you listen to your doctors—childbirth is quite manageable. From the Net I learned that if you just listen to yourself and your body, write a birth plan and use a midwife and a doula, giving birth can be a beautiful thing. And from class I learned that if you just make the right choices, you can create your ideal birth experience. I still instinctually held the opinion I'd formed as an eleven-year-old, that having a job was much easier than having a baby—but since I was already well on my way to the latter, I just resolved to try to make all the right choices.

So what would it *really* be like, this giving birth? The women I'd met who had only recently had babies were curiously tightlipped on the subject, and the women who had long been mothers could tell me only, "You'll know when you get there." But I needed more information. So I turned to the Web again, reading birth stories the way some people read romance novels. I read about women who labored for hours, only to have C-sections. I read about women who birthed at home, women whose labor went exactly as expected, and those for whom labor went disastrously wrong. I was still eavesdropping, in a sense, but this time I was privy to the full language of the discussion, the full disclosure of graphic details both universal and intensely personal. Still, even with all my reading and listening and imagining, I couldn't know what it was like until it happened. And when it happened, just like everyone had told me I would, I knew.

Birth of a Mother: Part 2

When it started, I was asleep. I was having a very vivid dream in which I was sitting on the side of a riverbank at night and there were candles floating on the water. As each candle came near me it seemed to glow brighter, and once it passed I'd look up to see the next one serenely floating toward me. As far as I could see down the winding river, there were candles, floating a few feet apart from one another, lined up like a string of stoplights along an empty street. Suddenly I woke up, realized that I was having contractions, that I'd been contracting throughout my dream, each real-life contraction peaking as a dream candle floated past me.

The contractions continued steadily for an hour or so, and I finally called the nurse line, excited and a little scared that this might really be it. It actually wasn't so painful; I remember thinking that if this was as bad as it was going to get, I was going to be in good shape. The nurse told me to go ahead and go to the hospital, so I woke up my husband and we hopped in a cab. At the hospital they secured me with straps and sensors to measure my contractions. Now, instead of a new-age vision of candles floating by, each contraction was marked by some beeping and a graph-paper printout of a line arcing and falling. Oh, yes: and my yelling.

Things were definitely getting more painful, but according to the resident who examined me, I was dilated only a single centimeter. Barely. So they had me walk around for a while, trying to hurry things along. We paced the hospital hallways, stopping every now and then to wait out a contraction, and after an hour I was examined again.

"Sorry, sweetie," said the resident. "You're going home."

"What?" I cried. "But I'm having all these contractions!"

"Yes, but they're not doing anything for you," she replied. "You're still just one centimeter. Believe me, you'll be better off at home. I'll send the nurse in to give you something to help you sleep."

I couldn't believe they were sending me home. The contractions were feeling pretty painful at this point, and my relaxing dream of candles floating toward me on the river now seemed laughably naive.

"But how am I going to know when I should come back? How will I know when I'm really in labor?" I asked.

"Oh" came the predictable response. "You'll know."

"Here," said a nurse, who gave me a packet of something. "This will help you get some rest."

"What is it? Will it hurt the baby?" I asked, gritting my teeth through another evidently unproductive contraction.

"No, it's just some Seconal. A sleeping pill. Try to get some rest."

A sleeping pill! How could they give me a sleeping pill? What if it hurt the baby? What if I couldn't wake up?

"Will it really knock me out?" I asked, getting a little panicky. "What if I sleep through it?"

"Sleep through what?" the nurse asked. "Labor???" And then she laughed for about ten minutes straight.

We went home, a little disappointed at the anticlimactic end to our hospital trip. And I felt not only the slight embarrassment of having so lamely outed myself as a birthing newbie ("Will I sleep through it?" Oh, if only!) but also an increasing sense that in terms of the pain level, at least, things were going to be getting worse before they got better.

After a long day of more contractions, all uniformly spaced and not increasing that much in intensity, I gave in to the doctor's suggestion and took the sleeping pill. No dreams that night, just the stupor of drug-induced sleep—until I was bolted awake by contractions so painful, it was all I could do to keep from crying.

I went to the living room. It was 2:00 A.M. I turned on the TV and half watched whatever was on, trying to distract myself from what my body was doing. It felt like the worst menstrual cramps, the worst intestinal cramps, and the worst diarrhea feeling all at once. The contractions were starting to come closer and closer to one another, and the pain was becoming more intense. Now I understood why the labor nurse had laughed at me. Sleeping through this was definitely not an option.

I called the nurse hotline and ended up speaking to the same nurse I'd talked to the night before.

"Oh, you poor thing!" she said. "I thought you would have had that baby by now!"

"Me too," I said, and started crying.

"Okay, wake up your husband again, and head to the hospital," she instructed. "And I'd better not hear from you tomorrow night! Good luck!"

I woke up Gil, who moved faster than I've ever seen him move in his life, and we grabbed our bags and hopped into yet another cab for yet another trip to the hospital. The cabdriver seemed a little nervous to be carrying such an obviously pregnant and uncomfortable fare in the wee hours of the morning. He drove faster even than cabs usually drive, probably praying the whole time he wouldn't be involved in delivering a baby in the backseat before the trip was over. We made it to the hospital by 3:00 A.M.

At the hospital, the night staff was unmoved by our sense of urgency and importance. They helped me to the table slowly; they hooked me up to monitor my contractions lackadaisically; they took their time and chewed their gum and didn't seem to notice my wrenching pain. It was my first realization that this—this laboring in pain, this bringing of a child into the world—probably happens every day tens of thousands of times all over the world. In any case, my own imminent delivery did not appear to be a novelty.

Finally a resident came and checked me, told me I was three centimeters dilated, and said that despite the unimpressive number they'd admit me to the labor and delivery floor. I was so relieved to not be turned away and sent home again that I almost forgot to be freaked out that all the pain I'd been withstanding had only brought me to only three centimeters, with seven more to go. I was admitted to a private room with a rocking chair, a shower, a bath, and a window. The pain was becoming unbearable, and each contraction descended upon me with an increasingly surprising force.

Throughout all my childbirth classes (and my informal online education), I'd held more or less fast to the conviction that I'd probably try to give birth without the epidural. When people would ask me whether I planned to have one, I'd tell them, "Well, we'll see how it goes. I'll try and labor as long as I can and if I need one by the time I'm seven or eight centimeters, then I'll get one." Another resident came in and checked me again. Still three centimeters. Would I like an epidural? "Please!" I begged. So much for "seeing how it goes."

The anesthesiologist arrived about twenty freakishly painful contractions later. I was never so grateful to see someone bearing a foot-long needle. He had me sit up in the bed and hunch over. "You realize you have a scoliosis of your lower back?" he asked me. "That could make this a little tricky." I nodded, but I was in too much pain to care about what he was saying. After several unsuccessful attempts, compromised by my jumping or otherwise moving during especially painful contractions, he finally inserted the needle and got the epidural working. Or kind of working. I only felt a little numb on my right leg, but that was such a wonderful relief I didn't question the fact that the rest of me still felt every bit of each contraction. Then, after a few minutes, neither leg felt numb. I kept pressing the little button they had given me to activate the painkiller, but nothing was happening.

The anesthesiologist returned, saying my curved back was the problem, and tried again. Again, no respite from the pain. This time only a two-square inch-section of my upper back got the effect of pain relief, which would have been fine if I was going to be expelling the baby from between my shoulder blades. After consulting with the nurses, the resident, and my obstetrician, the anesthesiologist delivered the grim news: the epidural wasn't going to work for me. I was caught between a feeling of panic and a feeling of resignation. Wasn't that what I'd told everyone anyway, that I'd try and go for it epidural-free? Well, now it appeared I would get that chance. I remember acutely the simultaneous clamoring in my brain of anxiety and acceptance, and the feeling of peace when I stopped panicking and let myself absorb the fact that I didn't have a choice: this baby would be born the way she would be born, and I would have to be strong enough to withstand it.

At around 8:00 A.M. the OB checked me and told me I was six centimeters and fully effaced. He asked me if I wanted something "to take the edge off" the pain. I was hesitant: would it hurt the baby? Would we both be drugged? I was assured that it would merely help me rest throughout this most painful part of labor. "It's 8:00 A.M. now," the OB said, consulting his watch. "I'm guessing you'll probably have this baby by, I don't know, four or five." Four or five??? I opted for something to take that edge off.

My memories of the next hour or so are of bolting upright with each contraction to yell, "It's not taking the edge off!!!!" and yelling at my husband, who was trying to be helpful: he kept watch over the contraction monitor, and every time he'd see the needle start to rise, he'd calmly say, "Oh look, here comes another contraction!" To which I'd reply, "YOU THINK I DON'T KNOW THAT???"

The pain seemed interminable, and I'd lost all sense of time. To me it seemed I was eternally contracting, growling, hyperventilating, and wrestling with my body. According to my husband, in between contractions I was drooling and comatose on the pillow, occasionally babbling some non sequitur before springing to life and screaming about the edge not being taken off. I felt as though it would never end, as if those candles I'd seen floating in the water were actually instruments of torture that stretched out into infinity. And then suddenly things changed.

• • •

Up until my labor, everything had been explained to me in similes: it'll feel like really bad cramps; it'll feel like the most incredible pressure; it'll feel overwhelming; it'll feel like you have to shit out a watermelon. When it actually happened, when I moved from interminable labor pain to active childbirth, it didn't feel like anything any simile or metaphor could ever come close to explaining. And yet that is the only way the experience can be described. Suddenly I had a contraction that was so intense it seemed like three contractions in one, both in duration and in pain level. It felt like a convulsion. It felt like the uncontrollable heave of your stomach when you are throwing up. It felt completely out of my control. The next contraction came almost immediately, and again I felt as though my whole body were convulsing. Then I realized: I was pushing.

For some reason, in all the books I'd read, classes I'd attended, and stories I'd heard, the pushing part had always been presented as something someone would be instructing me to do. In my mind I had envisioned that I would get to a certain point and then the regular hospital cast of characters would assemble around my bed and someone would tell me, "Okay, now, PUSH!" But that's not how it happened. My body was pushing, and I couldn't stop it.

Terrified that I was doing something wrong by breaking the rules and pushing without being told to, I frantically urged Gil to go get the doctor. I was equally afraid of getting in trouble for pushing on my own and of pushing the baby out with only myself and my husband there. It was 9:40 A.M.

The nurses and the resident came quickly, but it wasn't until they took a look and saw the baby's head that they started moving with the alacrity such a situation deserves. Everything became a blur for me. My memories from then on are just images and sounds. Suddenly the bed was converted into a delivery table. Suddenly Gil and the nurse were holding my legs and telling me to sit up and push. Suddenly my regular OB wandered in wearing black scrubs, looking weary, as though it were nearly ten at night instead of ten in the morning. My eyes opened and I was being told to push. My eyes closed and I was being told to try not to growl so much. Someone said, "Conserve your energy, push with your body not your voice." I discovered that I was powerless to push without my body's being ready. When my brain ordered a push independent of my body's contracting, I was just pushing, and nothing productive happened. When I pushed along with my body's convulsing, I was riding a wave, clinging on and resisting the urge to disappear into the undertow.

Suddenly, right when I thought I couldn't do it anymore, when I thought I'd be stuck forever in a miasma of pain and convulsions, I heard Gil say he could see her head. Someone told me to look down, and I saw the unreal vision of my daughter's head sticking out of my body. She looked utterly unfamiliar to me, a stranger's face, with a perfectly round head and delicate features, not the wrinkly little-old-man newborn I'd expected. I was told not to push. My eyes opened and I saw a gleaming metal tray of instruments. Something loosened and her shoulders were eased out of me. She wasn't crying.

"Why isn't she crying?" I asked. "Shouldn't she be crying?" I heard words strung together in what must have been sentences. "Possible meconium . . . don't want her to aspirate . . . clean her first . . . " Then she was out. Gil cut the cord. I saw her for a brief moment before she was whisked off to a far corner of the room. I kept asking why she wasn't crying.

Then my eyes closed and the OB was pressing my abdomen. My eyes opened and he was handing the placenta to someone who was taking it away to do research. They leaned their heads together at the end of my bed. "Looks small," they said. Then suddenly I was being sewn up. I felt every stitch, and it was painful. My OB said, "It'll be over soon." My eyes closed and my OB told me I had a second-degree episiotomy. My eyes opened and he was gone. I was on the table alone, crying. Everyone was crowded around Emily in the corner, a million miles across the room. A nurse noticed me crying and came over to ask me if I was okay.

Then, amazingly, Emily crying, Emily in my arms, looking like a beautiful stranger. Gil crying, kissing me, telling me I was the best kisser ever. Emily looking around, calm and serene, with seemingly alert eyes. Someone taking a picture of us, the first picture of me and Emily together. In the picture, which we managed to get developed only weeks later, I am tear-stained, exhausted-looking, distraught. We are both wearing our hospital-issued garb, me in what is unironically referred to as a hospital gown, one shoulder of it falling off as if I am trying to be casually fashionable; Emily snug and warm-looking in a knit hospital baby hat, bundled and bundled in layers of crunchy-feeling white blankets with pink and blue stripes around the edges. I cradle her as if I am unsure how to hold her. I am looking at the camera with an expression that is simultaneously overjoyed and overwhelmed, while she is serene in my arms, gazing up at me clear-eyed, unemotional, and calm.

Afterwards, in the relative comfort of my hospital room, my baby unbelievably snuggled next to me instead of inside me. I was exhilarated, full of adrenaline, weepy at the sight of her, incredulously proud of both of us. I felt superhuman; I felt as though I had accomplished some incredible physical feat, as though I had run the longest marathon and climbed the highest mountain and swum the farthest distance and won every event in the Olympics all in the same day. My sense of accomplishment was only slightly diminished by hearing news reports of a woman who, the same day I delivered my baby, was trapped in a flood and gave birth alone, in a tree. It was a tantalizing thought that for just a moment, despite the fact that I most certainly had the advantage in terms of medical support, comfort, and probably balance, we were sisters, bound by our common experience of childbirth. We had made it through the initiation process, she and I and women in homes and hospitals and possibly trees around the world, whether we used epidurals or had C-sections or "natural" deliveries. We had made it through to the other side. We were mothers.

I realize now why women tell and retell their stories of labor and childbirth. It is an incredible experience virtually unparalleled by anything else a person might endure. The vocabulary around it belies its emotional and physical intensity, perhaps to lull us into imagining that this rite of passage is more manageable than the reality of it seems: "giving" birth, "delivering" a baby. As if birth is something you hand over of your own free will, a package you sign for. It is not quite as domesticated as that, not so benign and painless, not so divorced from the realm of the physical, the primal. So now I understand the whispers and the hush and the similes and the metaphors surrounding it. Now I have confirmed my initial instinct that having a baby is much harder than having a job. Now I am ready to join my mother and her friends at the table, sharing stories of pain and love and triumph over a pitcher of orange juice and vodka, lowering my voice in deference to those around us who may not be ready to hear the full magnitude of our shared experience.

Misconceptions

The first time I was pregnant, I had no idea what was going on. I was weepy over commercials, shaky and dizzy if I skipped breakfast, prone to sobbing over a paper jam in my printer or a fax that failed to go through. Finally, realizing that in addition to all the hypersensitivity I had also missed my period, I took a home pregnancy test: two lines. Positive. It felt reassuring to know I wasn't crazy, just pregnant.

I was elated. We had just moved from New York to Philadelphia, where my husband was beginning medical school after a career on Wall Street. We had found a spacious apartment with a wonderful view. I had somehow managed to convince my bosses to let me continue my New York work from Philly, telecommuting from the comfort of my new bedroom. And now a pregnancy. It seemed perfect, all these new beginnings at once.

Just days after taking the test, my body already seemed to be changing. In addition to the emotional sensitivity, I was queasy, yet hungry—no, ravenous—all the time; my breasts were incredibly sore; I was already gaining weight, changing in shape. I was carrying a secret inside me. After a week or two we told my husband's parents. The next day I lost the baby. I have always been terrible at keeping secrets.

I woke up that morning and discovered I was bleeding. Even though I had read that some bleeding could happen and that everything still might be fine, I was sure it wasn't a good sign. As the morning progressed, the bleeding became worse, and I knew in my heart it was over. I sat on our new bed, in our new apartment, looking at our new view, crying my eyes out and wondering what, if anything, to do. New to town, I hadn't even set up an appointment to see an OB. New to the endeavor of pregnancy, I had no idea whether I needed to go to the hospital or simply let things happen as they happened. My husband was unreachable, sitting in some classroom somewhere, diligently scribbling notes as he listened to his professor lecture on embryology.

I managed to remember, in my confused and sad state, that one of his good friends from college, who had taken the direct route to becoming a doctor, going straight through school instead of detouring through another career, was working as a physician somewhere in town, so I tracked her down. I called the hospital where I thought she worked, somehow managed to talk a nurse into giving me her emergency pager, managed to wait until she finally called me back, and then choked out the words to communicate to her what was happening. She told me what by then I reluctantly already knew: that I was losing the pregnancy, that there was

25

nothing I could do. She told me to rest, to call her back if the bleeding got worse. I cried to her over the phone, telling her I couldn't understand what was happening, why it was happening. I told her that even though it had only been only a few hours since the bleeding started, I was already starting to lose my "pregnancy feeling"—no more swollen breasts, no more nausea, no more.

"I know," she told me. And as it sunk in that she meant more than just sympathy, that she really *knew*, she repeated it. "I know." How could she know? Until I experienced it myself, I had no idea miscarriages were so common. True, I had leafed through Gil's embryology textbooks and marveled that babies were born at all, given every minuscule thing that had to go right in order to create human life. But still I hadn't realized how, for lack of a better word, *ordinary* it was for an early pregnancy to end in miscarriage. My husband's friend and I shared our stories with each other, and though I still felt sad and confused, I felt a little less alone.

As strange as it had been to be pregnant—with my body taken over by uncontrollable urges—it was stranger to no longer be pregnant. The bleeding continued like a long, heavy period. Every once in a while I would feel nauseated and it would hit me that it wasn't because I was growing a life inside me but because I was losing one. Every once in a while I would get a hunger pang, and it would remind me of the intensity of my hunger during those few fleeting weeks. Yet I do admit to feeling a guilty relief at being back to myself.

I was still sad, though. I knew intellectually that I hadn't lost an actual baby—a moving, thinking, feeling thing—but merely the beginnings of such a thing, yet I still felt grief, I still felt loss. I was somewhat jarred out of this when my boss happened to call me during one of my weaker moments. I told her, through tears, what had happened, and her upbeat response was "That's great—at least you know you can get pregnant." What was she talking about? I thought. But then she told me: she had been trying to conceive for years with no luck. From her perspective even a spontaneously aborted pregnancy was a positive sign. "This one wasn't meant to be; it was off; there was something wrong with it. It was a misconception," my boss told me. "Just be glad your body knew what to do with it. Don't be sad about it, just try again. Really, it's for the best."

I remember being struck by two things: one, the marvel of our bodies' secret lives, the personal revelations I suddenly heard as a result of my own loss, the stories everyone seemed to have that I never knew before. And two, the dawning realization that things might not be as simple as I'd imagined when I first thought it would be a fun thing to get pregnant and have a baby. What if it happened again? What if I did manage to get pregnant again only to miscarry at eight weeks, just like this time? What if, like my boss, I found that I was unable to get pregnant? What if I was infertile? What if my best efforts at motherhood were effectively thwarted by my own body?

A week after my miscarriage, a friend came to visit. We spent a lot of time just walking around town, exploring the neighborhoods, talking about people we both used to work with and the restaurants we used to go to. I spoke a little about what happened with my brief foray into gestation, and she reassured me the way a good friend does, offering sympathy and a completely unfounded assurance that next time everything would work out fine. Our long walk through town took us to the Philadelphia Museum of Art, where we admired the Van Goghs and the Eakinses, and I lost myself for a little while in the satisfaction of looking at beautiful things. Before we left, we hit the contemporary wing, where there was an installation on display.

"Oh my God, look at that." My friend pointed, and, obediently, I did. I was caught off guard by what I saw.

It was a room full of what looked like fruit, oranges and bananas and grapefruit carefully laid out on the floor. Museum patrons were allowed to interact with the exhibit, and the sight of casually dressed tourists tiptoeing around the fruit, careful not to disturb it, peering closely and in some cases taking pictures, made me laugh out loud. Then, as we came closer, I saw that it wasn't just fruit strewn about the room, it was *dead* fruit. Rotten bananas, oranges, and grapefruits gone soft. As I walked even closer, I saw that the fruit was not merely decayed: each piece had been carefully hollowed out, the rotted inner flesh scooped and scraped away, and the outside peels stitched up to make the fruit appear whole again. Some were sewn up with thick, brightly colored yarn, the kind used to tie bows in little girls' braids. Some were held together with thread in fanciful cross-stitch patterns. Some were laced with surgical stitches. Some had glittery buttons, some had jaunty bows. As I finally came into the room, I found myself crouching to the ground with the rest of the tourists, unable to stop myself from touching the yarn and bows and buttons, the futile attempts to infuse the dead things with life again.

My friend put her hand on my shoulder as I sat on the floor of the exhibit, unable to stop myself from crying. She told me, "It's called 'Strange Fruit'."

Two weeks after my miscarriage we went to a friend's voice recital. I said hello and made small talk with everyone, never letting on about the truth of what had happened inside my body. I scanned the crowd for women, mothers, grand-mothers, wondering how many had a story like mine. How many of us had invisibly nurtured our own strange fruit? How many of us had stitched up our grief with optimism?

On the way home, I helped Gil study histology by reading him his lecture notes, a strange, polysyllabic vocabulary of reticula and haemopoiesis and mesenchymal something-or-others. I read aloud for the entire two-hour trip, and at some point in the middle of the B-cells chapter I felt a distinct pain on the lower right side of my body, near my hip about where my right ovary would be, according to the pictures. I'd never had pain around the time of ovulation before, but I'd read about mittleschmerz and I had a fair idea that this dull aching, this tightness, was the sensation of an egg's being released, a message from my body that it was time again. The sensation lasted almost the whole evening, through the rest of the car ride, through our having sex, through dinner with a friend, through the walk home. I felt like the pain was deliberate, a message, someone tapping me on the shoulder and whispering, "It's time for me to be born."

Two weeks later, I was pregnant again. At my first ultrasound, at seven weeks, roughly around the same time I had miscarried the first pregnancy, I was halfway convinced they were playing a videotape of someone else's visit, so foreign did it seem that there could really be a living creature inside me. I was so worried there would be only an empty sac there, and at first that was all I could make out on the little screen, without my glasses. But then, as the picture began to take shape, I could see a little piece of fuzz clinging to the top of this blob, which they informed me was the gestational sac. The doctor said, "There's your baby!" and zoomed in closer. Then all of a sudden that little fuzz was pulsing with life; we could see the whole shape of it flashing with its heartbeat. My husband squeezed my hand hard and I started to get a little choked up from realizing it was real, from the relief of finding it to be real, from the sheer terror of it being real.

Then the doctor asked us if we wanted to hear the heartbeat. At first, there was just silence as the tech tuned the equipment, and I was sure I wouldn't be able to hear anything over the sound of my own heart, but after a few minutes the whole room was enveloped in sound: whoosh-whoosh, whoosh-whoosh. The doctor took some measurements and then looked around inside, checking my ovaries. He found the corpus luteum on the right, which meant that the egg came from the right ovary, exactly where I'd felt that surprising pain. We left the appointment with our little shiny ultrasound picture, our first picture of our first baby, proof that it had really happened, that it was really there.

I kept that picture with me like a talisman, looking at it every time I was dogged by the fear that this pregnancy, too, would be lost. This time I felt the tenuous nature of my endeavor, the unsettling knowledge that at any moment it could be taken from me. My misconception, my miscarriage the first time around, was an abrupt introduction to the pure essence of parenting: the intensity; the joy; the grief; the fear of loss; the surprising connection to other people; the incontrovertible fact that the life you have created is simply out of your hands, beyond your control, beyond the scope of any other experience. It readied me, in ways I could not know until I was finally there, for motherhood, for the powerful rush of love and other overwhelming emotions, the depth and breadth of which I mistakenly thought I already knew.

Mother Love

When I was first married, I taught piano out of our home. One of my students was a woman named Jeannie, who had received the gift of piano lessons and an upright Yamaha piano to practice on— in celebration of her fiftieth birthday. So nervous that she had her husband call to arrange her first lesson, she was nonetheless excited about finally having the chance to fulfill a lifetime goal of learning to play. At her first lesson, she perched on the bench as if she weren't really supposed to be there, sitting gingerly on the edge, her feet on the floor, ready to run if need be. She couldn't bring herself to actually touch the keys.

"Your piano's so beautiful," she told me. "I don't know if I can do this."

"Sure you can," I told her. "Just press a key down and it'll make a sound. That's all it takes."

She brought her right hand up, let it hover close to the synthetic ivories, and finally dropped it back to her side. "You don't understand," she said. "I really can't do this."

"Okay," I told her. "We don't have to play right away. We can just sit here. We can talk about playing."

She laughed. "I know it sounds ridiculous, but I just can't bring myself to play even a note. You don't understand—you're so young, younger than my kids even." She turned to me. "This is probably the first thing, the first thing *ever* in my life that I've done that's just about me. The first thing I've ever done for myself as an adult, the first thing that's not about my kids. I don't know how to explain it to you, but I just feel like if it's not for my kids, I don't really deserve to be doing it."

We talked for a while about what a big deal it was to learn something new, especially as an adult, and how empowering it could be to learn the piano, an instrument she'd always wanted to play, just for herself, for no one else. She admitted that her kids had gone in with her husband on the gift of the piano and lessons, and I got her to reluctantly agree that possibly, in some small way, then, taking lessons and playing really *was* about doing something for her kids, not just about doing something, selfishly, for herself. It wasn't until she convinced herself that the lessons would benefit her kids as much as herself—by making them happy that she was enjoying their birthday gift—that she could bring herself to depress a single key.

Week after week, she made progress, from being able to touch the keyboard at her weekly lesson to finally admitting she'd gotten up the courage to take the dust cover off her own piano and actually play a few notes at home, alone. Soon she was able to play a few easy melodies, and her joy over her accomplishment was infectious. "Oh, my kids aren't going to believe this!" she'd tell me after successfully making it through "London Bridge."

As her lessons progressed, I heard more about her children, about her life as a young single mom, raising them on her own. She told me stories about what it was like in her neighborhood with two kids in diapers, living in a four-story walkup, juggling work and trying to be around to tend to her kids' every need. She told me about her parents and her relatives, how her father forbade her to go to college, and how determined she had been to make a better life for her kids. At fifty, she was petite and energetic; I could only imagine her intensity as a young mother, the necessary effort it must have taken to do everything that she did and still have a huge Italian home-cooked dinner on the table every night without fail.

By the time she was able to play a simple Bach minuet— an amazing achievement for a woman terrified to even touch the keys at her first lesson—we had moved beyond a teacher-student relationship. She was a mother figure to both me and my husband, bringing us food, giving us recipes, and crowing over our individual accomplishments. I looked forward to her lessons as much for the excitement of watching her make such great progress musically as for hearing more stories of her life of willing sacrifice as a mom. It was something utterly unfamiliar to me.

She somehow managed to fit the stereotype of the martyred

mother, giving and giving of herself until there was seemingly nothing left, without actually being that stereotype. She wasn't claustrophobia-inducing or clinging; she hadn't driven her kids away—on the contrary, they loved her and seemed to reciprocate her exhaustive efforts at making their lives better. The cards they sent her for Mother's Day and her birthday were heartfelt and sentimental, not the printed Hallmark ready-made pap with a hastily scribbled signature that I might send if I remembered. She was selfless without being overbearing, loving without being suffocating, supportive without being cloying. She was a mystery to me, the kind of mom I'd heard about but never imagined actually existed.

When I became pregnant with my daughter, Jeannie's stories and experience took on a more practical relevance for me. I had so many questions about what mothering would be like: What does it mean to love as a mother? Is it all selfless sacrifice, giving until you have nothing left? Or is it enough just to love and have a little of yourself left over? Is it food on the table every night, doing something special for your child's birthday, leaving little notes in her lunchbox? Or is just being there enough, giving your baby a roof over her head and clean sheets beneath her as she sleeps? Would I fall in love with my baby at first sight the way I'd heard I should? What if I didn't? What if I couldn't? What if I loved her but she couldn't love me? The most troubling part of all those questions was that until my own child was born, I could answer them only as a daughter. The deeper question of how I would be as a mother could not fully be answered until I already was one, already loving or hating, succeeding or failing, or otherwise living through those questions. I wanted to be more than just a "good enough" mother, but could I really be like Jeannie? Could I be that selfless? I worried I was far too selfish to do what she had done, that I was too selfish to make sacrifices, too childish to do what it seemed mothers need to do. And yet, if I really was too selfish, too childish, how was I supposed to be a mother? Are mothers even allowed those kinds of feelings?

A few days after I came home from the hospital with Emi, I sobbed in my bed as the postpartum reality hit that I was irrevocably, permanently a mother. Gil came in, concerned. "Do you want me to do something?" he asked. I couldn't stop crying. "Yes," I managed to choke out. "Call Jeannie."

Though it had been years since we had stopped our lessons, with my moving to Philadelphia and her moving to upstate New York, we still kept in touch. In those early postpartum weeks we spoke often. She became my role-model mother, in a sense. When things seemed too incredible, too overwhelming, I'd remind myself: if Jeannie did it on her own, lugging two kids up four flights of stairs on her ninety-five-pound frame, washing out two sets of eternally soiled cloth diapers ten times a day, doing laundry without a machine and cooking big Italian dinners, then I can do it here, in my elevator building, with my helpful husband, disposable diapers, and one kid. If Jeannie could forge a healthy family from scratch, so could I.

When she was finally able to come visit when Emi was two months old, she was reassuring. "You're doing great, hon," she told me. "You're a natural." When I confessed to her that I wasn't sure if I was cut out for motherhood, that I didn't know if I could love the way a mother was supposed to love, she told me, "Of course you can, sweetie. Look at her, look at this little darling. What's not to love? She's gorgeous, she's perfect. She's just like you." She gave me a hug and told me, "Listen, we all just figure this out as we go along. There's no textbook, there's no rules, there's no right way to love her. You just feel what you feel, you just love her the only way you know how."

I was reminded of the intensity of what I had felt in the delivery room after Emi was born. When my daughter was handed to me for the first time, when I finally had her in my arms after all those months of wondering and waiting, I felt the way I imagine Jeannie must have felt finally sitting at her very first piano lesson—excited, afraid, unsure of what to do, unsure of the ability to do it. When I finally held my daughter, the sense of simultaneous panic and relief was overwhelming. For until I physically touched her, I hadn't fully realized the enormity of what we both had accomplished: she had been born, I had birthed her. There was so much that could have gone wrong but didn't, and the fact of our both being alive and healthy made me feel as though we had escaped some deadly fate, at least for the time being. I felt overpoweringly grateful for the very fact of her, unworthy of our mutual health, undeserving of having made it through relatively unscathed. Perhaps this was the mother love I had been wondering about, this ferocity of thankfulness, this intense imperative to protect her from whatever the world may have in store, this determination to honor the horrible what-could-have-beens by making the most of what is. I did not fall in love with my daughter the instant I saw her the way I had heard other people do, the way I had seen it portrayed in the movies. I marveled at her, at the incredible realization that it was up to me to take care of her, and I felt myself silently pledge to protect her at all costs. Perhaps this was what love was. Perhaps, until I got the hang of it, that kind of love would be enough.

"You just love her the way you do," Jeannie told me. "And she'll love you right back, you'll see."

It was difficult to believe that in the early days of motherhood. In the beginning, there was no reciprocation, no response, just spit-up and burps and dirty diapers, no way to know if anything I was doing was forging some sort of love connection. My baby's range of emotion was crying or not crying. Used to more complexity, I tended to equate that with not loving or loving. "Please don't cry," I'd plead with her. "I love you." But she never seemed to hear me. I was convinced she wasn't connected to me, sure she seemed happier with other people.

When I look back at the videos we shot back before she had discovered free will, I am struck by how obvious and intense her connection to me appears. I am struck by how even at barely three months her eyes follow me frantically when I move out of the frame, how her whole body quivers at the sound of my voice. Now I can see what I couldn't then: how attached she was, how clearly I was her whole world. I see myself on camera acting the part of the mom and I remember how I wondered at the time whether she could see right through me, so afraid that she might not connect with me. And yet there it is on camera, despite all my ambivalence, all my doubts to the contrary: her absolute devotion, right from the start.

In some ways love is easier as my daughter gets older. For one thing I have more feedback, more proof that my love is reciprocated, in her spontaneous declarations of "Mommy, I love you so much!" or "Mommy, I love your green eyes." Of course, in some ways, in retrospect, it was easier to love when she was tiny, speechless, and helpless, unable to stubbornly refuse to go to bed on time or throw a public tantrum when denied something she wants. But I am learning as I find my way through the extremes of selflessness and fear that mothering and loving is complex at every stage, a tangled clutch of intense emotion utterly different from any adult love I have experienced.

Jeannie's break away from motherhood into piano lessons was every bit as tenuous and unfamiliar as my induction into motherhood and away from my normal, un-selfless life. Seven years after her first lesson, Jeannie is less conflicted about devoting time and energy to practicing piano, about the un-kid-focused joy she experiences when she is finally able to play the Moonlight Sonata. In fact, her piano lessons led to other risk-taking lessons. She has gone back to school to earn a college degree, something else she never imagined doing. And three years after my first introduction to motherhood, I, too, am less conflicted, able to embrace the complexity of loving as a mother without being dogged by fears of failure, of rejection. Jeannie's piano lessons were lessons for both of us.

"How's my little doll?" Jeannie asks of Emily when she calls these days. "Still amazing? Still beautiful? How could she not be with a great mother like you? Don't you just love her so much?"

And I do. Powerfully, incredibly, more intensely, and more selflessly than I ever could have imagined.

Pretty on the Inside

M y baby is beautiful. I know all mothers say that, but in this case I swear it's the truth. Store owners offer her balloons, bread, candy; people yell at us from their cars at stoplights; waiters comment on her charisma; old people get teary-eyed just at the sight of her. Her beauty is astonishing in the manner of all beautiful things: it is riveting, it is engrossing, the mere fact of it magnetizes whoever is looking. And perhaps the most astonishing thing about the fact that she is beautiful is the fact that I am not.

When I was pregnant, my husband and I joked about what our baby might look like if she were unfortunate enough to possess all of our least desirable physical traits. It was not a pretty picture. A double chin, a pointy nose, excess back hair, and, of course, the dreaded thigh problem. But in truth, when I thought about the potential of the new life growing inside me, it was always in terms of her intellect: how smart I imagined she'd be, how wise, how precocious. So imagine my surprise when she burst out of me perfectly formed, no smooshed head, no wrinkly little-old-man

newborn face: she was a true beauty. Her physical flawless-
ness was not something I could have ever predicted, and in
the first few days we spent together it was all I could think
about: how beautiful she was, how perfect, how appealing.
My husband was similarly awestruck. "How did someone
like this come from people like us?" he asked me, as if she
were a different species entirely. Shrugging our somewhat
sloping shoulders and scratching our less than perfectly
maned heads, we grappled with the heady realization that
the two of us had indeed had some major part in creating
the cutest baby ever.

I thought I had conquered my secret yearning to be beautiful. In high school I had been the shy, silent figure on the
fringe of the social scene, wearing black, writing depress-
ingly bad poetry, beneath it all wishing to have perfect hair
or Guess? jeans or whatever it seemed would catapult me to
acceptance. I wasn't exactly ugly, but I was no supermodel
either, and in high school that distinction is not so subtle. I
imagined that if I were only pretty, things would be different and the torture of my teenage years would be trans-
formed into the "best time of your life" scenario my
sociology teacher, the school's football coach, was always
claiming high school to be.

I did give it a shot one year: tried to buy the right clothes
with my baby-sitting money, tried to have the right hair and
makeup, tried to hang out with the right people. My foray

into the world of the beautiful people was short-lived when it was revealed that I had no aspirations to try out for the cheerleading squad. The most powerful, beautiful girl in the inner circle I was slowly infiltrating sneered at me, "You'd never be a cheerleader anyway. You'll never be anybody." It was small comfort then to envision that in ten years those same cheerleaders would be stuck in the same town, married to the same guys they dated in high school, envious of me and my totally different trajectory. And it was no comfort at all to hear from my parents that I was pretty "on the inside."

College was an improvement: I was interacting with people who cared more about what was inside my head than how it was packaged, and finally I felt like I was on an even playing field. Sure, I was still "the best friend," the "funny" one, the girl guys would go to to ask how best to approach some other, more desirable female. But I wasn't reliving the painful days of high-school social hazing either. I focused on things other than my non-beauty. I read Naomi Wolf's *The Beauty Myth*. I became politicized. Eventually I met someone who really did think I was beautiful and we got married. I believed my days of obsessing about being beautiful were behind me.

Cut to the birth of my daughter. In the beginning, her beauty was literally marvelous: I could have stared at her unblinking until my eyes dried up and rolled out of their sockets. Later her beauty was revealed to be a valuable evolutionary trait, as the irritation and possible ill will my husband and I would feel toward our baby upon being awoken miserably in the middle of the night dissipated at the sight of her sheer adorableness. Even with fifteen months of her beauty behind us, I still never tire of looking at her, I still marvel at her perfect features. I feel beautiful by association, and I imagine that her beauty can undo every bad thing caused by my non-beauty. I imagine that her beauty can grant her every opportunity I missed—that she will be the girl with all the right clothes, the girl who gets voted prom queen, who will never stumble or stammer or have an awkward moment, who will never have to suffer the shame of being picked last for softball, never have to be snubbed, never have her heart broken.

Perhaps my imaginings are the fantasies of a completely biased parent: perhaps at fifteen months she is as cute as any baby can possibly be but at fifteen years she'll be a little more average. But what if she really is gorgeous? Will her experience of growing up beautiful make her more like every shallow beauty who laughed at me in high school, every trend-mistress who ridiculed my clothes, every entitled cheerleader who crushed my feelings with easy dismissal? My rationalization for not being pretty was that my character was being built. So if my daughter never experiences the heartbreak of being un-beautiful, will she still have character? Without the desperation of desiring acceptance, will she still become the brave, compassionate, intelligent woman I imagine she'll grow up to be? If her life is made easier because of her beauty, will she never be forced to examine the more complicated aspects of her soul?

I know I will have to be careful as my daughter grows older and becomes conscious of the fact that beauty matters in this world. But for now, while I still can, while she is still a baby, I soak it up: I bask in her beauty; I tell her how amazingly gorgeous she is; I stare at her eyes as if they are architecture, as if they are works of art. I steal these moments now; later, when she is old enough to understand, I will try to tell her there are other things of more importance. At this point I still don't know the totality of my daughter as a person: who she is, what she thinks; whether she has inherited my husband's aptitude for standardized tests or my fear of failure, my quickness or his hesitation. But for now I revel in the fact that by some quirk of genetics she has been formed into a combination of our best selves, presenting to the world the beauty on the inside I always hoped was really there.

Separation Anxiety

The night before my fifteen-month-old daughter's first day of playschool, all of us parents met with the teachers to discuss the upcoming Big Day: our babies' first day of "school." The meeting was basically a pep talk. "Your kids will cry when you drop them off, and they will cry when you pick them up, just to confirm your fear that they have cried the entire time you were gone," the head teacher told us. "Don't worry—they haven't. Just try to leave on a high note, make your goodbyes short and sweet, and let us deal with the tears. The crying lasts only as long as you stay."

It sounded simple enough, and in fact Day One was easy. My daughter couldn't get to the toys fast enough, pushing me out of the way so she could get both hands on the Legos. She didn't even notice I was leaving, even after giving me kisses and saying "bye-bye." Although I was glad to see her so well adjusted, I felt perversely hurt—couldn't she shed just one tear to make me feel even a little necessary? Couldn't she cling just a little bit? I left feeling slightly dazed by my toddler's willingness to say goodbye to me.

Day Two was more difficult: my little girl said goodbye without hesitation, but when she saw me leave she began crying. "Okay," I thought, "This is more like it. A few tears, a few hugs . . . at least I know she'll miss me a little when I'm gone." Day Three was when it really hit her that when she goes to school, Mommy leaves. Though she was still excited to see the classroom, the teachers, and the other children, she cried as soon as I set her down. We looked at some books together and I tried to help her become absorbed in an activity she liked, but still she clung and implored me not to go. When it became clear that I was in fact leaving, she stopped crying "Mama! Mama!" and instead started calling out for her daddy. That's when I started crying. One of the other moms came over to gently remind me that I was only prolonging the agony by staying and by allowing myself to become upset. "Be brave," she told me. "Just say goodbye." I got myself together, said yet another goodbye, and left my daughter to fend for herself.

Aside from feeling embarrassed that I had let my emotions get the best of me, I felt a little sheepish about my earlier wish for my daughter to express some sadness at my leaving. I should have encouraged her budding independence, I chided myself. I should not have undermined her excitement with my own mourning of the passing of her babyhood. In the clear absence of emotion, it all made perfect sense: my daughter looks to me for cues as to how she should act in certain situations. If I am sad or fearful or anxious, she might interpret that to mean she should approach the situation with trepidation, learn to be cautious, learn to be doubtful. When I am happy, cheerful, or confident, I help give her the confidence to face new things. But this is so much easier said than done. How can I smile, how can I encourage her, to do something new, when secretly I am terrified of what she might discover? She might get hurt, she might think I've abandoned her—or worse, she might realize she doesn't need me as much as I need her. Must I really hold my breath and stand aside as she navigates the cement steps at the playground or awkwardly tries to scramble up the slide? Must I steel myself to smile and not run to her side as she begins to explore the world around her on her own? Must I merely watch as she becomes less mine and more the world's?

When my daughter was first born, I couldn't stand to be apart from her. I missed being pregnant, and after nine months of carrying her with me, as a part of me, everywhere I went, I felt as though something was missing when she wasn't in my arms, snuggling next to me or dozing on my shoulder. In the early postpartum days, in the thick of the baby blues, I found myself weeping over everything and nothing, and the only thing that made me feel better was holding her. So I held her as much as I could and even slept with her beside me. This attachment, this need to be with her, was the flip side of my ambivalence, my worries about mothering in general, and it was just as powerful. As Emi grew bigger and I adjusted to the shock of no longer being pregnant, my need for her diminished, but only slightly. She was with me, on me, almost constantly, and I felt as though that arrangement was reassuring for us both.

The first time I had to leave her, taking a two-day business trip to New York when she was a few months old, I missed her terribly. It was thrilling to be back in my old life, working and doing things just like I used to do, and yet it was strangely discombobulating to be walking around without her in my arms or in a stroller in front of me. Throughout the day, sitting in my old office, I'd suddenly panic that I'd forgotten to feed her. Throughout the night, I'd wake up, convinced I could hear her cry in the sound of the hotel air conditioner. At one point, walking around the Upper West Side, I saw a woman crossing the street with a baby, and my stomach dropped the way it might if I were on an amusement park ride: it contracted deep inside the way it had in the early postpartum days at the mere sound of my baby's cry. It was a purely visceral reaction, and the intensity of it caught me off guard. I couldn't get home fast enough, and I remember when I finally made it back to the apartment, it didn't bother me that Emily apparently had not noticed my absence in the least. I just held her, smelled her baby scent, cradled her for hours. I never wanted to let her go.

Months into playschool, drop-offs and pickups are relatively uneventful. Our partings are no longer such sweet sorrow:

for the most part my daughter is happy to see me leave and happy when I return. She talks about school on the days she is not there, and if she does get a little clingy at goodbye-time, I know that it is a temporary situation, one that will quickly resolve itself after a big smile and hug from me as I leave her.

This is only the beginning, I know. I will feel the pang of separation when she is two, when she is twelve, when she is twenty. My daughter will tackle other more important milestones, other more difficult accomplishments that she must achieve on her own. And I, who once shared a blood supply with her, who once had her all to myself, must wait and watch and smile, and continue this exploration of motherhood, this bittersweet experience of maternal love, this continual process of bravely saying goodbye.

II

Mother Shock

〰〰〰

Crisis. Initial differences in language, concepts, values, familiar signs, and symbols lead to feelings of inadequacy, frustration, anxiety, and anger.

—Kalvero Oberg

Irritation and Hostility. After the initial excitement is over . . . the initial curiosity and enthusiasm [can] turn into irritation, frustration, anger, and depression. Minor nuisances and inconveniences lead to serious distress. Symptoms experienced during this phase include: homesickness, boredom, withdrawal, need for excessive amounts of sleep, compulsive eating or drinking, irritability, exaggerated cleanliness, stereotyping of or hostility toward local people, loss of ability to work effectively, unexplainable fits of weeping, physical ailments.

—Whitman College's Web site on culture shock and studying abroad

Why should I get dressed? I had thought bitterly, when every three hours I have to get undressed to nurse? Why should I comb my hair, when soon it will be filled with spit-up, and lines of watery shit, dried and smelling, will run like little rivers down the front of my shirt, while on my shoulders, like the golden pads of old military glory, will be the white marks of a successful burp?   —Jane Lazarre

Throughout pregnancy and nursing, women are urged to relax, to mime the serenity of Madonnas. No one mentions the psychic crisis of bearing a first child, the excitation of long-buried feelings about one's own mother, the sense of confused power and powerlessness, of being taken over on the one hand and of touching new physical and psychic potentialities on the other, a heightened sensibility which can be exhilarating, bewildering, and exhausting. No one mentions the strangeness of attraction—which can be as single-minded and overwhelming as the early days of a love affair—to a being so tiny, so dependent, so folded in to itself,—who is, and yet is not, part of oneself.   —Adrienne Rich

I was so tired. Now I wonder how I did it. I swear young mothers are equipped with some sort of juice or hormone that enables them to bear it.   —Doris Lessing

Giving Birth to Ambivalence

The first thing I can remember thinking when they handed me my daughter seconds after her birth was "Who is this little stranger?" She didn't look like me, she didn't look like my husband; she was a tiny, perfectly formed human being, and even though I saw her completely round head, her delicate fingers, her long toes, and her calm eyes, I couldn't connect this little person with the faceless kicks and jabs I had felt inside me for so many months. I knew enough to expect that my delivery would not be the stuff of *A Baby Story,* all blurred-out yucky parts and love-at-first-sight happiness. I was still surprised to discover that my first emotion was not the intense love I'd heard described but, instead, a sense of overwhelming responsibility.

People said to me when I was pregnant, "Oh, your life is going to change!" as if they were not stating the obvious. My life had already changed—I was pregnant—and when it came time for the baby to be born my life would change again. What they didn't tell me was exactly how it would change or the ways in which it would change me. I knew to expect sleepless nights; I knew to expect crying; I knew to expect exhaustion; I even knew to expect joy. I didn't know to expect ambivalence. I didn't know to expect doubt.

For the two days I spent in the hospital recovering from my delivery, I was on an adrenaline high. We had too many visitors to count, and I welcomed them all as they cooed over our new daughter. The baby and my husband stayed in the room with me, and a wonderful staff of nurses nursed us through our first tentative days as parents.

Things changed when we got home. I hadn't gotten more than four hours' sleep in the two days I was in the hospital. I was so sore it felt like I'd been run over by a truck. And the inevitable hormonal roller-coaster had begun as my body did its job of adjusting to no longer supporting another life. I became extremely weepy and cried over everything and nothing—catching a glimpse of my non-pregnant body in the mirror; getting out of bed the way I used to when I was pregnant and then suddenly realizing that I no longer had a huge, weighty belly to maneuver around; putting on a pair of sweatpants I wore for the last month of my pregnancy and being shocked when the waistband snapped back to fit so loosely on my stomach. I missed being pregnant, and I cried all the time unless I had my baby with me. I held her the whole time I was awake and slept with her in my arms. Nearly every time I dozed off I dreamt she was still inside me, kicking, only to wake up and find myself cradling her next to me.

But I had read the books, I knew what to expect about those first few weeks. It was normal for me to have "baby blues." I'd get past it. And so when people said to me, "Isn't motherhood just the best thing ever?" and "Do you just spend all day kissing those little baby toes?" I said what I was supposed to say. Which was that I loved every minute of it, that I didn't mind one bit being sleep-deprived, that being a mom was the greatest thing in the world. I figured eventually I really would mean those things.

I jumped right back into my job. Since I was working from home, I figured, how hard could it be? I found out soon enough. I learned the hard way not to underestimate the stress of trying to negotiate being both a new mom and a good employee. Immediately and constantly, I felt torn by the demand of deadlines: who comes first, the client or the baby? Faxing those galleys or changing that dirty diaper? Either choice meant failing one or the other.

I began to have insomnia. Once my daughter woke up in the night I would be up for hours, lying awake and beating myself up for not being better at this mothering thing. Why did it seem so easy for everyone else? Why was it so difficult for me? I had been used to doing difficult things, but I had been used to succeeding at them. I never imagined it would take a little six-pound baby to bring me to my knees.

I felt helpless, I felt overwhelmed. I wished things were back to the way they were when I was pregnant, when being a good mother basically just meant remembering to take my prenatal vitamins. Things were so much easier when we shared a body: I could be a mother without knowing how to mother, I could take care of my baby without having to worry if what I was doing was right or wrong. I didn't realize how terrified I was of failing at mothering, failing my daughter, until one night when my husband asked me for the 150th time that hour, "Do you think she's okay, do you think she's still breathing?" And I thought: what a relief it would be if she weren't okay, what a relief it would be if she were gone.

It was a horrible moment, a horrible thought, and I instantly felt like a horrible mother for thinking it. I felt a sickening kinship with those mothers and fathers you hear about on the news and read about in the papers, parents or caregivers who snap, who shake or hit or leave or hurt their babies in a fit of insanity or desperation or plain old sleep deprivation. Before I was a parent I would think, "How could anyone hurt her own child?" But here I was with a good-natured baby, a supportive husband, a nice apartment with a washer and dryer—here I was with seemingly everything made easy for me, and yet I still felt awed in the face of responsibility, I still felt like I couldn't handle it.

I had terrible fantasies. Driving home from the grandparents' house, I would half imagine/half hope that my husband would swerve our car into the huge semi next to us. I would, in a fit of desperation, envision the horrible crash that would ensue and experience for a moment the fleeting sensation of relief that all of this—this being a mother—would be over.

One night when I couldn't sleep, I lay awake planning in detail my escape: I would pack a small overnight bag and slip out at 3:00 A.M. No note, no message. I'd just leave. I would go to the ATM and take out as much cash as I could. I would walk over to the bus station at 11th and Market and take the bus that went farthest. I couldn't go to New York, nor New Jersey nor Boston nor California; those were all places my husband would think to look for me. I would go somewhere nameless, faceless, some small town in the middle of some unheard-of place, where I could have no identity and just start over. I would get a job waitressing. I would live in a motel. I would do whatever it took to make some money to live on, and I would sleep all night. My time would finally be my own. I drifted off to sleep, eventually, lulled by the fantasy of escape. In the morning, I remembered my midnight plan and told my husband, laughing at how ridiculous it sounded in the light of day. I expected him to be a little horrified, but when I finished telling him my secret scheme, all he asked was "Were you going to go by yourself or were you going to take the baby?"

I kept telling myself, everyone does this, everyone survives it. Women give birth and become mothers every day, right here in this city, in cities I've never heard of, in cities around the world. I was one of an endless succession of women going through that profound physical and emotional transformation every day. The thought was both humbling and encouraging. How did mothers mother back in the fourteenth century? Did they talk about feeling helpless, did they talk about feeling lost? How about Victorian mothers? Did they suffer the indignities of their postpartum bodies in private, were they entirely alone in their experiences? And what of mothers in underdeveloped countries, mothers living on the edge of poverty in our own country? Women have been becoming mothers since the beginning of human history, I kept reminding myself. If they can do it, I can too.

Eventually I cut my work hours to part-time. Eventually I found other new mothers forging their way through similarly emotional territory. Eventually I began to doubt myself less and trust myself more. Eventually I began to mean it when I'd say sure, yes, being a mom is the best thing ever. My insomnia gradually disappeared and my baby started getting into a routine, napping in the day and sleeping for extended stretches through the night. I felt more like my old self, less like I had crossed over into some strange place I was not prepared to enter.

One day when my daughter was about four months old, I was in the park with her. She was sleeping, I was reading. I was feeling good, feeling happy, feeling confident. A family walked by us, a tall man holding hands with a little girl who looked to be about eight, a woman walking just behind them. They stopped and looked at my sleeping baby and we had the standard conversation—how old she was, how much she weighed, how much she slept. I smiled and they smiled back and they went on their way. A few moments later, I was surprised to the see the woman hesitate and turn around to come back to where I was.

"Do you see that little girl there?" she asked me, pointing to the girl I had assumed was her daughter. "That's my granddaughter. That man holding her hand is my little baby. He's thirty-eight now, but he's still my baby." I told her she didn't look old enough to have a thirty-eight-year-old baby, that I had thought she was the little girl's mother. She shook her head and smiled at me. Suddenly it looked as though she had tears in her eyes, and she reached down and squeezed my hand. "I just wanted to tell you," she whispered, "it gets better. It gets so much better from here."

I think about her a lot, especially when things are better. How brave of her to tell me, how thoughtful of her to sense I needed to hear that. She couldn't know, of course, how badly I needed to have someone reassure me that I was a good mother, that it's tough at first for everyone, and for all she knew I could have been offended by what might have seemed an assumption of my incapability. But she told me, and I often tell the story of her telling me to other new mothers I meet.

"It gets so much better from here," she told me.

She was right.

Loving Every (Other) Minute of It

I was catching up with a friend the other day, someone I hadn't spoken to in a while, who is now a new mom. She asked me what I was doing these days, so I told her that I've been writing a lot about "the dark side" of motherhood that isn't talked about much. "You know, the stuff you don't read about in the magazines," I told her. "The things we'd really like to talk about when someone asks us how it's going, instead of saying what they want to hear from us, which is that we're just loving every minute of it." She laughed, she told me she thought that was just great. Then I asked her how she was doing with her barely three-month-old baby, how she was adjusting to being a mother, and she replied—with a complete lack of irony "Oh, I just love every minute of it."

I suppose it's not surprising that so many mothers fall back on this standard answer, since we're basically given two options for motherhood: good or bad. There is not a lot of room for any ambiguity, and it doesn't make much sense. In other areas of our lives—in our jobs, in our marriages, in our relationships with our family members—it's perfectly acceptable to experience the full range of human emotions, from happiness to satisfaction to frustration to resentment to blissed-out, heart-soaring love. Complain about your taskmaster boss and nearly everyone can sympathize. Talk to a friend about a distant spouse or a frustrating relative and you have a shoulder to cry on. You can like your job but hate your boss, love your spouse but mourn what you feel is lacking in your relationship, care about a family member but not want to spend a whole heck of a lot of time with her. But mothers are placed in an emotional straitjacket. We have limited options—unconditional love or unspeakable abandonment—and many moms find that discussing with others their ambivalence about their children or their parenting abilities results only in blame, guilt, and in some extreme cases a covert call to child protective services.

Nearly every mother I know wrestles with this in some form. It's rare that I can talk to another mom about the difficulties inherent in what we are doing without one of us mollifying the situation by quickly saying, "But it's all worth it" or "But I wouldn't trade her for anything" or "But really, I just love every minute of it." As mothers we are quick to disown our anger and ambivalence, even over something as simple as normal, acceptable frustration with our everyday lives. It is as if we feel that acknowledging our very human reaction to what's taking place completely eradicates any other emotions we may be feeling—like, for instance, those good emotions we're supposed to have exclusively. Well, I don't have any feelings—good or bad—exclusively, and I don't know anyone who does.

Becoming a mother is a complicated thing. Not only am I trying to negotiate a relationship with my child, a relationship that defines itself as it becomes defined, I am trying to negotiate a relationship with myself as I attempt to determine how I mother, how I feel about mothering, how I want to mother and how I wish I was mothered. Having become a mother, I have also become a part of something larger than the maternal dyad of myself and my daughter: I am now a member of a new society, a new demographic, a new cultural category, with all the weight of our society's ideas of motherhood upon me. I am sorting out how I mother my child, how my mother mothered me and how I fit in with the world's idea of what a mother should be, and that is no small task. It's also not something I can do without ambivalence, conflict, or emotion.

As I try to navigate this new terrain, I'm slowly learning that feeling conflicted does not mean that I don't love my child. I'm coming to realize that the ubiquitous magazine and media portrayal of the ever-loving, always-happy über mom is an expression of that childish hope we all harbor for the perfect parent rather than a prescriptive formula I must follow. I'm slowly convincing myself that experiencing what I'm really feeling is better than forcing myself to "love every minute," which only breeds resentment toward this tiny person who somehow rules my life and refuses me the complexity of human emotion. It's still difficult to admit to myself that I don't actually love every minute of what I do from day to day without immediately wanting to take it all back and try to be the Good Mom, the perfect blank slate onto which others can write their own impressions. I try to remember that I was psychologically complex pre-motherhood and that no one thought I was a bad person because of it.

It's harder than you think to admit your even occasional dissatisfaction as a mother without feeling instant guilt, an immediate sensation of shame for even suggesting you might not be happy when you've got a wonderful healthy child in this world who depends on you and loves you no matter what. It's almost impossible to separate your "bad" feelings about the normal frustrations of post-baby life from your "good" feelings about the very baby who instigated the transformation. But it's not realistic or healthy to deny the fact that a mother is a complicated person—or to deny that a mother is a person at all.

So let's imagine for now that our love for our children and our thankfulness for their existence is a given. Let's imagine that no one can possibly doubt the depths of our feelings for our sons and daughters. Let's imagine that everyone in the world knows exactly how much we love all the many things there are to love about our children and the relationships we have with them. Let's imagine that we are all most definitely Good Moms, and, with all that on our side, admit for a moment what we don't love. I'll give you my list, you add your own.

I don't love every minute of going to the playground.

I don't love every minute of going to the museums.

I don't love every minute of watching Elmo.

I don't love every minute of having to wake up early in the morning.

I don't love every minute of having interrupted sleep at night.

I don't love every minute of having to be the one to make the rules and the one who must enforce them.

I don't love every minute of laundry.

I don't love every minute of changing diapers.

I don't love every minute of having to endure the stares of people when my child freaks out in public.

I don't love every minute of making food that my kid ends up throwing on the floor.

I don't love every minute that I have the Barney song stuck in my head.

I don't love every minute of having to reason with a tantrum-throwing toddler.

I don't love every minute of being peed on, pooped on, and thrown-up on.

I don't love every minute of weaning.

I don't love every minute of sidewalk chalk.

I don't love every minute of having to pick up the blocks fifteen times a day.

I don't love every minute of putting my life on hold.

I don't love every minute of tantrums.

I don't love every minute of going to story time at the library.

I HATE the Teletubbies.

I don't love every minute of being chained to someone else's routine.

I don't love every minute of not being able to go to the bathroom without company.

I don't love every minute of being a mother.

Does reading that make you feel bad? Guilty? Itching to protest that it's all worth it? Desperate to reassure yourself that you couldn't possibly feel that way, that you really do love being a mother, all the time, every waking moment?

I know. It's hard. But it's not such a horrible thing to give ourselves permission to be human. And maybe the next time someone asks us how the whole mom thing is going and how much we love it, we can be a little more honest with ourselves and tell them, "I just love every *other* minute of it."

The Invisible Woman

I can actually see it happening: at a bookstore I ask for a book with the word "motherhood" in the title and the assistant's eyes glaze over. I meet someone at a business lunch and at the mere mention of my twenty-month-old daughter the conversation quickly dies. Over and over I am greeted as if I am a normal, interesting person, and then once it becomes evident that I am a mother, I immediately become less appealing, more easily dismissed. Even childless friends who used to ask me how this or that project was going now say, "So how's that whole mom thing working out?" People who might be interested to know that I once performed a solo piano recital at Carnegie Hall or that I graduated as valedictorian of my college class and had my master's degree by age twenty-two excuse themselves from the conversation before they can discover any of those things about me, because they have already found out all they need to know: I'm a mother. I am in Elmo's World, not theirs.

Before I became a mother, I was ambivalent about having children precisely because of this seemingly inevitable process of becoming invisible to the rest of the world. Pre-child, I was guilty myself of making the same assumptions I now find others making about me: that a mom is not quite a person, that a mom is someone who can think only about playgroups and poopy diapers, who lives vicariously through her kids, who doesn't have a real job, who totes around a giant purse containing everything from wipes and crushed Goldfish crackers to sippy cups and slobbery teething rings, running from here to there to make it to soccer and music on time and still be home with enough time to slap a nutritious dinner on the table.

How hard could it be to be a mom, anyway? Before I had my daughter I assumed it was surely not as difficult as meeting multiple deadlines and managing complex projects. Surely not as challenging as troubleshooting and problem-solving in the office. Surely not as daunting as working a sixty-hour week. I would be able to handle it; I would be able to do it all. I would not become invisible. No, I told myself, it would not happen to me: I would have children, but I would not become a mom.

Until you have crossed over the painful threshold of birth into the dark side of sleeplessness, selflessness, and the complete atrophy of the person you had thought of as yourself, you cannot presume to know what it is like to be a mother. From the other side, it is all so clean and simple: having a baby is a choice and mothering is easy if you just manage it the way you approach your job in the "real world." The problem with that, of course, is that it's not as simple as choosing, and motherhood is not a job at all. It is a full-time, all-consuming, life-subsuming career with no pay, no stock options, no social security, and lots of lip service with little actual respect (just watch the difference in people's reactions to you when you tell them you are a project manager instead of a mother). It also does nothing to pad a résumé, as women discover when they attempt to reenter the working-for-pay world. So my naive plan to be in the world of motherhood but not of it didn't even come close to working the way I thought it would. I discovered soon enough that you cannot have a child without becoming a mother, and I also found to my dismay that within months I had become one of the invisible moms I swore I'd never be: I was forced to reduce my working hours to care for my daughter. Women who could have been my peers looked right past me and my stroller on the street. Construction workers didn't even exhort me to smile. It had become official.

My new status was reinforced by the boss who disappointedly remarked that in choosing to stay home with my child I had made it clear I wasn't committed to having a career; the friends who unknowingly belittled the tremendous transition from woman to mother by reminding me that my conflicting emotions around mothering and invisibility were just "baby blues;" even the free parenting magazines, coupons for diapers, and junk mail about baby life insurance that suddenly flooded my mailbox. Was I no longer someone who could be described as committed? Had my intelligence suffered from having given birth? Had even my personal target demographic narrowed to the suffocating niche of mommy magazines and baby superstores? I had been grateful to find that my old favorite online read, Salon.com, had a "Mothers Who Think" section, which made me feel a little more connected to the world I existed in before I was a parent. But then I discovered that "Mothers Who Think" has officially been renamed "Life," which was perhaps an attempt to include thinking mothers in the realm of universal day-to-day existence, but, in effect, rendered invisible one respectable place on the Net where it was clearly acknowledged that not only do mothers have brains, they actually use them.

How hard can it be to be a mom? Now that I am one, I know. It's extremely hard. And it's also hard to communicate the true difficulty of day-to-day maternal life. Often, it's only when you break down the multitude of tasks into a list of discrete, recognizable, real-world accomplishments that you can fully grasp the scope of what mothers do. Consider one study that estimates a mom simultaneously and often single-handedly performs as many as seventeen occupations in the course of raising a child, from child-rearing, cooking, cleaning, chauffeuring, and financial planning to resolving family emotional problems (not to mention often doing part-time paid work in addition to it all). That particular study estimated a mother's worth at $508,700 a year, according to

Ann Crittenden's *The Price of Motherhood*. Of course, mothers do not get paid anything close to that figure, since they are not paid for their work at all. Mothers, particularly mothers who stay at home with their children, have traded their economic viability to invest in the invaluable creation of human beings. You'd think that would be empowering. You'd think that would be respectable. You'd think that would be an interesting point of conversation. You'd be wrong.

Love is its own reward, say the kind of people who look right through me as my daughter and I pass by them. How can a person compare having a 401K plan with actually being there to witness her baby's first steps? How can anyone measure personal autonomy against the cries of a helpless infant who has no choice but to love and trust its caregiver? How can someone say they would trade any of that for a nice title, a big office, and the respect of her peers?

Well, not everybody has to. Only mothers. And as long as it's only a mother's trade-off, it doesn't merit much attention. Mothers can be as invisible as mothering itself, the skill that is hardly noticed in the patient soothing of a sick baby; the tactful negotiating of a battle of wills between toddler and sibling; the consistent presence of nutritious food and safe shelter; the gentle daily direction and guidance of which a child and dare I say the rest of society?—is barely aware.

Our sons and daughters may be your doctors someday. Our children's work might pay your retirement benefits.

Our babies may one day run the companies that grant your grandchildren six or more months of paid family leave and the right for both parents to return to part-time positions with full benefits and on-site childcare. So don't ignore us. Don't look past us. We're right here, in front of you, doing the most important job a person can ever do.

Mother Shock

I remember the first time it hit me that I was actually married. We were on our honeymoon, at a bed and breakfast in Newport, Rhode Island, and the front desk called up to our room.

"Hello, is this Gil Binenbaum?" a voice inquired.

"No," I said, "that's my, uh . . . I mean, he's my, uh . . . " I couldn't think of the word. He wasn't my boyfriend, he wasn't my fiancé, he was my . . . my . . . well, we were married now, so that meant he was my. . . . I could barely bring myself to say it. Finally I blurted out the h-word to the guy on the phone. *Husband*. That meant I was somebody's wife. It sounded so old-fashioned, so middle-aged. Wasn't it just the summer before that I was supporting myself, living alone, reading Susan Faludi's *Backlash*? How could I suddenly have a husband? How could I suddenly be a wife?

It was with a similar shock that the news sunk in again and again after Emi was born that I was a mother. "Congratulations!" someone would say over the phone that first week post-delivery. "How's your new daughter?" My mind would race. Daughter? The word confused me. How could

I have a daughter? *I* was the daughter. No, wait, that's right: I'd had a baby, and it was a girl, and that meant . . . yes, I had a daughter. And she was fine. "Oh," I'd say after having reasoned through the logic, "She's fine, she's great," reminding myself, Emily is my daughter; when people ask, that's who they're talking about. "And how's Mom doing?" people would say next, and I, not realizing the third-person inquiry was about me and not my own mother, would reply, "Oh, she's doing great, really happy, first granddaughter and all that." Then I'd realize they meant *me*. It was just like when I was pregnant: people whom I'd just met would ask me when I was due, and, thinking they had asked me "What do you do?" I would respond with a lengthy explanation of my job description before realizing from the slightly confused looks on my listeners' faces that I had completely misunderstood. It took a while to adjust to the fact that the mom in question was now me, the daughter people spoke of was this baby of mine. The generational seating chart had shifted by one, and I was sitting in a new place, my little girl now occupying the spot where I used to be.

When my husband started medical school, he was concerned about how being an older student would affect his ability to compete with his fellow classmates. "Don't worry," a friend told him. "Don't you know that old joke? What do you call the worst student who graduates from the worst medical school in the country? A doctor!" The same joke could work for a new parent: What do you call a woman who has just had a baby, whether or not she has any experience, knowledge, or innate maternal skill? A mother! In the beginning it just didn't seem right that I should have the same title as someone like my friend Jeannie, who'd had nearly thirty-five years' experience as a mom, or my mother-in-law, who'd raised two kids, or my own mother, who'd raised three. And yet I did: even just hours after delivering my first baby, the nurses would ask me, "How are you feeling, Mom?" or "How are Mom and baby doing today?" It seemed almost disrespectful to the millions of mothers who had actual experience and hard work to back up that designation. Shouldn't I start out the way I did when I took my first editing job, as an assistant, and work my way up? Wasn't there some sort of hierarchy? Maternal Assistant, then Assistant Mother, then Associate Mother, then Mother, then Senior Mother, then Managing Mother, then Mother-in-Chief? It just didn't seem right, jumping headfirst into this new job with the same title and daunting responsibility as someone who had done it for years.

I felt as though any moment someone would see through my inexperience and confront me on it, and the imagined scenario would always end with her taking my baby away and giving her to an actual mother, someone who really knew what she was doing. I tried my best to take the kind of advice espoused by television self-help gurus and just "fake it till I make it," going through the motions of mothering with confidence I didn't yet have. I walked through the park with my baby just like a real mom. I fed my baby just like a real mom. I rocked my baby to sleep just like a real mom. I changed diapers and gave baths just like a real mom. I got up in the night again and again just like a real mom. Eventually, I reasoned, I'd become so comfortable acting like a real mom that I'd actually turn into one.

The anxiety I felt as a new mother certainly wasn't any pretense, however. Giving birth to my daughter had made me some sort of flashpoint for all the joy and suffering in the world. I couldn't watch the news without crying over someone's missing child, a family's misfortune, a deadly car wreck. I'd hold my little baby tight, feeding her as I wept over late-night commercials about starving children or stories of mothers who had lost their babies to senseless accidents or terrible diseases. I simultaneously experienced ferocious love and horrible fear for my daughter, a rush of thankfulness undermined by the suspicion that we were undeserving of having made it through safely thus far.

I imagined the kinds of things only new parents understand imagining. When she fell asleep soundly the way babies sometimes do, I worried she might never wake up. When she stayed awake for hours longer than usual, I imagined she'd never again fall asleep. Walking with Emi in the Baby Björn I'd envision myself tripping and falling, crushing her beneath me. Pushing her in the stroller, I'd picture a car careening out of control at an intersection, knocking us down and pinning us to the asphalt. Feeding her, I'd foresee her choking and me unable to save her. I began to half believe that if I could imagine all the horrors of what might happen, I might be able to eliminate the possibility of any of those things actually coming to pass. What would I do if she lapsed into a coma? What would I do if our cat attacked her? What would I do if there were a fire in our building? It became a habit, almost, the conjuring up of deadly scenarios to counteract the possibility of their actually occurring. Even when I realized this magical thinking wouldn't stop fate from transpiring, wouldn't make me a more experienced mother, I couldn't stop imagining the what-might-bes. I managed to find danger in the most mundane things. Walking in platform shoes, I'd imagine myself tripping. Standing in the kitchen, slicing up greens for a salad, I'd see my fingers chopped off, wriggling among the arugula.

Of course, living with a med student didn't help. Gil had similar new-parent fears, but he also had an incomplete medical education to back them up. Her cheeks look red—she could have Fifth's disease! She has baby acne—no, wait, it could be measles! She has reflux—she could have a severe malformation of her gastrointestinal tract! She occasionally looks cross-eyed—she has strabismus! Every fear I thought I could discount he could back up with half-understood medical references from textbooks not written to soothe the hyperactive nerves of novice parents.

And just when we both began to calm down, to realize our baby would most likely not be killed by our holding her the wrong way or by some obscure but deadly ailment, Gil had to start catching up on the material he'd missed in school when she was born. He began studying at home, reading lecture notes online and viewing videotaped classes on endocrinology. I'd sit in our glider, watching the tapes with him as Emi slept in my arms, my apprehension coming more and more strongly out of remission with each mention of some dread disease that manifests only years after a baby is born. There were illnesses that showed up only when a child hit puberty, for instance, or biological imperfections that could go unnoticed until early adulthood. There was one congenital disorder wherein a normal-seeming girl would suddenly turn into a boy, growing male genitals at around the time she should be starting to menstruate (*huevos doces*, "eggs at twelve," is the nonmedical name for it). There were other things, countless other things, that could go wrong, that could show up out of nowhere in a child that seemed otherwise to be the picture of health. My husband learned from his lecture tapes and notes the details he needed to know to successfully understand endocrine diseases and pass the class; I learned that even the appearance of health and safety don't necessarily guarantee the absence of danger.

This was the true initiation into parenthood, the sudden frightening realization that I had a fragile life to nurture and no reliable, infallible means of nurturing it. I wanted to protect my baby from all the dangers of the world, and yet until she was born I hadn't realized the true scope of danger. But my anxiety over this was actually a way to limit my focus, to restrict the overwhelming possibilities of what might happen into a more comprehensible, if still fear-inducing, list. If I was worried about tripping and falling with her, I could put her in the stroller. If I was afraid of being hit by cars at intersections, I could be on the alert and exercise caution. If I was afraid of her choking, I could take an infant CPR class. I could find productive ways to address those fears, and by doing that regain some measure of control—control that could make me feel more self-assured in the face of all the possible things beyond it.

As I moved up in my own mind from Assistant Mother to Associate Mother, mastering some of the more panic-inducing new-parent anxieties and feeling more at home in my routine, I began to feel less like I was acting the part of the mom and more like I deserved the title. Eventually I realized I wasn't always tempting fate just by taking Emi for a walk or stroll around the park or otherwise acting as if life was something we could take for granted. My anxiety receded as my confidence grew, and I saw that the more comfortable I felt in my new role as a mother, the less I needed to conjure up terrifying circumstances to justify my fears.

The decisive moment for me was when I was able to apply those new, odd-sounding designations of "mother" and "daughter" to myself and Emi without hesitation. Once when Emi was nearly six months old I was out with her and my in-laws, shopping in a department store. An older lady came up and peeked in the stroller where Emi was sleeping. I protectively stepped closer, fixing Emi's blanket and moving her bunny out of the way.

"How old is the baby?" the woman asked.

"Almost six months," I told her.

"That's right," my mother-in-law joined in, "Next Thursday will be six months! What a milestone!"

The older woman smiled and looked at me. "Well, aren't you a dear," she said, "helping your mom take care of your new baby brother."

"Oh, no," I said without even thinking about it, "It's a girl. And I'm her mother. She's my daughter. I'm the mom."

For the first time, it didn't feel completely strange to say it, to admit to being a mother. I said the words, and more than that I meant them, and I'm not sure who was more elated at that moment: me for finally feeling as though I deserved to publicly proclaim myself a mother, or my mother-in-law for being mistaken as someone young enough to be the mom of a six-month-old baby.

I still have my moments. There are still days when I am shocked to remember that I'm a mother now, that I'm the one who's supposed to soothe the boo-boos and know what to make for dinner. But I'm slowly getting used to it, slowly finding it normal to be the mother of a daughter instead of the daughter of a mother. And now when I hear a little voice calling "Mommy!" I don't always have to look around to see who that means. I'm starting to know it's me.

Motherly Advice

As much as I was hungry for information about how to be a mother when I was pregnant, I hated receiving unsolicited advice. I couldn't stand how people assumed I would do the same things they did, and I resented being told how I would feel about mothering. Everyone, it seemed, had an opinion that I needed to hear, and often everyone's opinion was different. "Take it from me," people would say. Or, "Let me tell you," they'd begin. Whatever they said would always end with some piece of vital information that would doom me to eternal bad parenthood if I ignored it.

Once my baby was born, the endless parade of advisers continued. I was told by old ladies on the street that my daughter was overdressed or underdressed, or that she wasn't wearing a hat and would be cold, or that she was and would be hot. After fighting and losing the sock war with my baby, concerned strangers would point out to me, as if I simply hadn't noticed, that my child wasn't wearing any socks. After pushing the stroller for miles trying to induce a nap, I would be surprised out of my own half-sleep state by the loud voice of someone telling me "helpfully" that my daughter didn't look very comfortable. ("Is she asleep? Then she's comfortable," became my standard, sharp-toned response.)

Grandparents had their ideas about things, friends with and without children had yet more ideas, the pediatricians and book experts too. Give her a pacifier, no don't ever give her a pacifier. Put her in a crib, no let her sleep with you. Start her on solid foods and she'll sleep through the night; no that's a myth, don't give her anything solid yet. Put her on a schedule, no let her dictate her own schedule. Let her cry, no pick her up. Whatever decision I made seemed to contradict someone else's expert opinion, and eventually it was less exhausting to just nod and smile than it was to fight their firm stand on whatever it was I was doing wrong.

Most disconcerting was the advice I'd get from women, older and therefore wiser moms, whom you might think would be more compassionate. "Come on, newborns are easy!" they'd say as if I were a wimp for suffering the effects of sleep-deprivation. "Get that baby on a schedule!" as if she were a train I had to catch. "You've got to show her who's boss!" as if she were a dog I had to train. "Don't let her start running your life already; there's nothing worse than a kid who's in charge of the parent." As if I had a choice.

The unsolicited advice from strangers was the post-partum equivalent of the belly rubs they felt compelled to give me when I was gestating. Now my baby, not just my belly, was public property; now my mothering, not just my body, was open for public commentary.

What I heard people saying to me was "I know better than you. You won't be able to do it your way, your way won't work, your way isn't good enough"—which is the wrong thing to tell someone stubbornly bent on perfection. But perhaps if I was able to get past my own insecurities about the choices I was making and my irritation at being told what to do, I might have heard that what everyone was saying had very little to do with me.

My husband's family loves to give people directions. Often the discussion over how to get somewhere takes longer than the actual driving time, but that's fine with them. They could debate the merits of the turnpike versus the parkway all night if need be, and it is rare that we can make our exit after a weekend visit without a rundown of which route we're taking and how bad the traffic is. I had a good friend in college who swore that every time he was out in public, someone would stop him and ask for directions. He believed that this was because he looked like someone who had a pre-ternatural sense of exactly where he was going, that he looked like someone who could tell other people how to get where they needed to go, literally and figuratively. I am usually silent during the in-law direction debates, and I rarely get asked for directions, but when I do, I feel a rush of what I imagine my husband's family and my old college friend must feel when called upon for their expert advice: I feel experienced. I feel wise. I feel magnanimous in my ability to point the way, generous in the sharing of my proprietary knowledge. I'm sure whoever is asking me how to get to 18th and Chestnut couldn't really care less whether or not my ability to direct them there gives me a feeling of empowerment, but it is undeniably there, rising to the surface as I point my finger and smile.

This is, I think, the rush of the advice-giver, and this, I think, is why the advice they give is more about their own personal issues than a real need to address some deficiency in me. The real information lurking deep below the surface of what they feel compelled to tell me is that their critical-sounding pointers really point to their own private regrets, their own unmet needs, the things they wish they could have done but for whatever reason did not.

When I was able to distance myself a little, to not take the advice quite so personally and instead think about it as a reflection of the advice-giver, I was able to become a bit more charitable in my responses. Instead of just getting irritated, I tried to imagine that every time I left the house with my daughter, I was suddenly acting a part in an overly cutesy foreign film where everything is layered with more meaning than it actually has, random events are portents for things to come, and the landscape is peopled with quirky characters whose seemingly mundane utterances actually contain hidden nuggets of wisdom, clues to the deeper meaning of life. When approached by strangers, I'd mentally cue up the whimsical accordion music and start inventing subtitles for what people were really saying.

"She's not wearing any shoes!" from a scandalized old lady became "I wish I'd been able to protect my children better." An old man booming "Look at that! Sleeping like a baby, eh?" loud enough to thoroughly destroy my daughter's chance for slumber translated to a whispered "I wish I'd spent more time with my kids." A woman helpfully pointing out that my baby would be spoiled by my holding her all the time had subtitles that read, "I am so afraid that I have failed my children." The mother telling me, "You have to show that baby who the parent is!" had a subtext that said, "I was so overwhelmed as a young mother by the feeling that my life was spinning out of control, I had to be strict, I had to be unyielding, and now I need you to be that way, because if you do things differently, if you coddle and cherish when I fearfully denied and ignored, and everything still turns out fine, then that means I have made a mistake, I have made the wrong choices year after year after year, and I can never go back and love my babies differently."

Imagining the advice as a kind of dialogue in need of translation helped me halfway believe that tangled up in all the well-meaning, annoying words was something important: the voice of experience, however poorly articulated. I could halfway convince myself of what I actually wanted to hear, which was that the strangers who tried to advise me were trying to communicate in the only voice they had that parenting is all-consuming, that mothering can be overwhelming, that we all struggle each day to make difficult choices under less than ideal circumstances. Giving people a more charitable voice made it halfway possible to believe that what they were trying to say was not that I was too idealistic or naive, but that life as a parent is more complex than anyone can possibly know, and that they had been there too.

Perhaps my creative listening, my attempt at responding with compassion to what actually irritates me, is merely an exercise. Perhaps those little old ladies or loud men or hardened mothers are merely speaking their minds, no subtext involved. Perhaps there really is no cutesy French film, no deeper sense of urgency, no extra meaning, no attempt at making a real connection in the guise of un-asked for, unwanted advice. But it makes it easier for me to hear it, to continue going in the direction I need to go, when I imagine that there is.

Fear of the Double Stroller

I'm not sure why it inspires such dread in me, why I shy away at the mere sight of a mother pushing a double stroller through the park, down the street, awkwardly through the doorway of one of the few stores in the city with an entrance wide enough to accommodate what seems to be the SUV of infant transportation. It doesn't matter if it's a side-by-side stroller or one of those where the babies face each other like passengers on a train or the kind where they ride one in front of the other as if on a roller coaster: it frightens me to contemplate, to imagine what it might be like to push around twice the cargo I have now. I'm not sure why. But unless the babies are twins (in which case the double stroller seems perfectly reasonable, an obvious choice given the circumstances), I think to myself, why two? Why isn't one enough? Don't those moms realize that the first one isn't finished yet?

My younger sister and I are thirteen months apart, an age difference that was great growing up because it meant having a built-in playmate in the house—at least until I reached an age where it was torture for me to be forced to drag her around when I went to play with other, nonrelated friends. Now having children that close together seems just plain unimaginable to me, a mother of a baby who, as I write this, is in fact thirteen months old. In the grips of postpartum madness during those early months, I asked my mother, "How could you have gotten pregnant again when I was only four months old?" I could hear her shrug through the phone, her memory of that time scrubbed free of hormonal imbalance, sleepless nights, overwhelming responsibility. "I don't know," she said. "We were just having so much fun with you we thought, hey, why not do this again?"

Her response seemed to me equally unfathomable and horrifying. Was I supposed to be having fun? I was not having fun. I was trying to work from home, loopy on Percocet, four days after giving birth; I was sitting on a stupid donut pillow to protect the hemorrhoids caused by pushing during labor; I was crying in the shower at my bloated new body; I was walking the hallways in the dead of night with a squalling baby on my shoulder, mentally cataloguing the contents of our medicine cabinets and wondering exactly how much Tylenol Cold it would take to make me sleep forever. When I went to my first postpartum checkup with my OB and she broached the subject of birth control, I told her, "No need to worry, I'm planning to never have sex ever again." It took weeks, at the very least, to adjust to a new worldview that incorporated a no-longer-pregnant me and a tiny stranger to attend to. I didn't feel like myself until at least three months after my daughter was born, and I certainly didn't regain even a reasonable facsimile of my pre-pregnancy body until months after that. How could I—how could anyone, for that matter—choose to go through the whole exhausting, life-changing ordeal again so soon?

But it was easy to brush off my mother's response: she's my mother, she's insane. What was more difficult was when moms from the playgroup started turning up pregnant. Every other week it seemed someone with a baby the same age as mine would walk in and announce the good news, leaving me hoping that the rapid draining of color from my face combined with my awkward stammering would seem to them an expression of my heartfelt good wishes. On the outside I said my congratulations, asked the usual questions, made the usual jokes, but on the inside my mind was boggling. *Are you crazy? Two under two? The second before the first is walking? A double stroller???* Some of them were admittedly freaked out by the news, but coping well. Others seemed to take it completely in stride: two down, one to go. Eventually I'd have to ask, my morbid curiosity getting the best of me. To the freaked-out newly pregnant ones I'd make it casual: "Wow, so you're gonna have to do the whole double-stroller thing, huh?" hoping my nonchalance would inspire from them a confession of their own stroller dread. To the ones who saw pregnancy number two as their logical step toward pregnancy number three, I'd ask, "So are you going to get the kind where the babies face each other or the one where they're side by side?" in a vain attempt to show exactly how comfortable I was with the subject matter, with motherhood, with the idea of at least two more years of diapers and strollers and runny noses and trips to the park resulting in the inevitable cuts and scrapes and disputes over other children's toys. No one ever responded with the same apprehension I felt toward the topic.

I should point out, in case my fear of the double stroller obscures this fact, that I love my daughter. She is the cutest, the smartest, the most adorable baby; impossibly bright, amazingly sweet; the most beautiful baby in all of Philadelphia and quite possibly the world. She is so superlative that to describe her leaves me sputtering clichés about bundles of joy and little angels, but the fact is that we walk down the street as if on parade, with her waving from her stroller like a beauty queen, and people stop, people smile, people stare. People yell at us from cars: "It's the Gerber baby!" "She's a living doll!" "So adorable!" (And once, mysteriously, "Hey, big daddy!") She can separate a shopkeeper from his wares before she's even halfway through her repertoire of tricks, and she can make your heart melt with her generous distribution of hugs and kisses.

So why do I get chills down my spine whenever someone asks me when the next one is coming? I have the OB telling me as he sews me up on the delivery table that next time it will go even quicker, so I should try to get to the hospital fast; the grandparents reminding me that having the baby toilet-trained early will make it easier when I have the next one; even my husband misting over at the sight of our sleeping girl, saying, "She's so wonderful! We have to make more!"—everyone, it seems, is acting as if this baby thing is a snap, a cinch, as easy as pie. I never, at one of my previous full-time jobs, had a boss tell me, "Well, you're doing great! Looks like everything's under control! In fact, you're doing so well, why don't you get another full-time job in addition to this one!" Why do people feel free to tell me to add another baby to the full-time baby I already have?

The double stroller looms as a physical embodiment of everyone else's hopes for me as a mother, that I'll have more babies, that I'll last through yet more postpartum blues, that I'll endure somehow still more countless numbers of sleepless nights. But for me, the double stroller means being right back where I started, sore and sleepless and stressed and confused and terrified of failing—but this time with the added pressure of another little pair of eyes to watch and learn as I cope or do not cope.

I think maybe I do want to have another baby, eventually, when I have more proof that things are turning out all right with the first one. But I worry about doing a good job; I worry about being able to do it all and do it well; I worry about having enough energy, enough patience, enough compassion, enough love. I worry about losing myself, about giving in to the snappishness I know lurks within me after nights of sleep-deprivation, about being a bad mom. If I never planned to have another baby, the double stroller wouldn't appear as daunting, and perhaps that's precisely what frightens me about it: that it could be my destiny.

My husband doesn't understand my double-stroller dread. To him it just makes sense: two babies to push around equals a stroller with two seats. But the way I see it, what's to stop me after the double stroller? Will it become a triple stroller, a quadruple stroller, an unending succession of multiple strollers? Will it become a lifetime of this uncertainty, this fear of screwing up another blameless person beyond repair?

I am kidding, of course; I know the double stroller is not the marijuana of strollers, the gateway to other, "harder" strollers. What I am wrestling with is what I suppose we all wrestle with as we try to fit into our new roles as parents. It's the balancing act I fear more than the stroller, I suppose: the balancing of mothering versus my old view of myself, parenting versus the pursuit of my own goals, the day-to-day-ness of what must be accomplished now versus the fantasy of what things will be like when strollers and high chairs and bibs are relics of earlier, more complicated times.

This week at playgroup one of the moms who just had her second baby shows up with the first baby in a stroller and the second in a sling.

Aha, I think.

There's an option.

Letters to Emi

When I went off to college, I received a letter from my dad. That might not seem like such a big thing, but at the time, it was. I was seventeen, I was far from home, and my dad was—and is—a very shy, private person. Many of our conversations when I lived at home consisted of my babbling endlessly to fill the silence and his saying "hmmm" every now and then. So getting a four- or five-page letter was a shock. Even more shocking, he wrote to me as if I were an adult, maybe even a peer. He wrote things about his life I never imagined him experiencing. He signed it not "Dad" but "Bill," essentially giving me permission to be a grown-up, and opening the door for a different kind of communication between us.

I couldn't write back right away. I kept imagining him sitting at work, getting out his graph paper at his desk, and trying to compose the letter. I kept thinking about how he never could have said aloud to me the things he wanted me to read. I was touched by his effort to speak to me. But I was overwhelmed. I didn't know how to respond. I kept meaning to write back, to let him know how blown away I was by what he had written, by the fact that he'd written at all. Eventually, so much time had passed between his sending the letter and my attempting to respond that it seemed easier to let it go, to not put pen to page and formulate into words this new status of adult-to-fellow-adult communication.

I wish I'd written back to my father. As a closet letter-writer myself, a writer of letters unsent, a writer of letters to myself and of overwhelming fifty-page letters I know some recipients must have tossed in the trash before even opening, I know how therapeutic letter-writing can be, and how much easier it is sometimes to write what you need to speak, how much easier it is to read than it is, sometimes, to listen. But eventually, I just called him on the phone instead, found the casual words to say thanks, glossing over the depth of what I really felt.

When my daughter was born, I was terrified of failing at motherhood. I was unsure of myself, convinced that everyone else knew what to do while I alone was clueless. I decided I wanted Emi to have a record of my good intentions just in case I really did turn out to be a vein of therapy for her in early adulthood, so I began writing a journal for her when she was seven months old. It is basically a series of letters about us as mother and daughter, roles that both of us are making up as we go along. One day, when she is much older, I will share this with her and she'll know a little better what my intentions were, no matter how things turn out. And I'll try to understand if she never writes back.

• • •

Monday, January 3

I had wanted to begin this for you on New Year's Day, to officially mark a new start or to make the beginning of this journal more meaningful in some way, but like so many things recently my intentions did not match up with my execution. I want to write this journal for you for several reasons, and I have put off writing it for several reasons as well. I have hesitated because although I have a monologue running in my head of what I want to say and how I want to say it, I know when I begin to write, it will all be different. I have hesitated because I dread the confrontation of my words upon the page; I cannot help but project to some future time when I will read through this and discover that the truth of our life conflicts so much with the hopes and good intentions I plan to describe. I don't know why I can't imagine that everything will be happy, I don't know why I assume there will be sadness and bitterness between us; perhaps I am just afraid of being a bad mother. . . . But that is also exactly why I want to write this journal for you: to remind me of what is foremost, that I love you and that that is what matters beyond all else; to remind me to have patience; and to make sure you know, unequivocally, what you mean to me. I don't want your experience of reading this to be the first time you realize how much I love you or that I love you at all; I just want you to be able to, someday, understand me—and, if things go badly, forgive me. I worried when I was pregnant that maybe I wasn't cut out to be a mother, and now that you're here, on the days when I am sleep-deprived and you are bellowing, I can see too clearly how close I am to being that bad mother I am so afraid of. So I write this for us both.

Sunday, January 9

There are so many things that will be lost over time, so many little things you do now that you will not do later. When you were first born, my favorite thing in the world was to hold you in my arms with your head on my shoulder and to hear your tiny, shallow breaths in my ear. You were so light I could carry you in one hand, and I did that a lot: you in one arm, me typing with the other; you in one arm, me loading the dishwasher with the other; you in one arm, me reading a book with the other. And your hungry mouth—surely that will disappear as you grow older. I can't even begin to describe how wonderful it is. It is the mouth you wear when you are concentrating on something intently, the mouth you have when your bottle is in sight and you are hungry, the mouth you get when you are gripping something in your chubby, tiny hands. How old will you be when you will just be hungry, without your hungry mouth to tell me so, or when you can concentrate without needing to summon all the energy of your entire face? Someday when you are hungry you will just eat, no hungry mouth, no diving at the spoon. So many things will vanish. And when you are older

I will not be the only observer: you will notice me, you will evaluate me as a mother, a role I am only interpreting as I go along. It is an ambivalent, interconnected relationship we share, a daughter who will one day be a mother, a mother who is still a daughter: we will know each other in ways we can never know ourselves.

Tuesday, January 18

Last week I noticed you opening and closing your mouth like a little goldfish. Playing by yourself, when you thought no one was looking, you'd shake your head no, then stop and open and close your mouth, open and close, open and close, then shake your head again—then smile when you realized I was watching. Soon you began to make sounds along with it, and suddenly you were saying "mama." Then two days later you woke up full of new consonants, saying "dada," "nana," "lala" and "blabla." You seem both bemused and excited by your newfound ability to make sounds that indicate meaning. And I'm realizing as you begin to explore this new skill, that you have been existing in a languageless world, unplagued by the search for just the right word; unable to express, in a way that everyone else can understand, exactly what it is that you want. What are your thoughts like if they are not in words? How do you experience the world? What *is* your world? I imagine you bombarded by sensation: seeing, hearing, touching, tasting; a jumble of sensory input. And yet I know these things are organized by you in some way: you can respond to the sound of your name in the midst of all kinds of other sounds; you recognize the layout of our house, the restaurant I often take you to; you know where the mirrors are that you like to look in and where the boxes are that you like to open. So you must somehow have thoughts, you must somehow have logic; somehow it must make sense to you, even if you are not thinking, "this is my room" or "This is that box."

Your first successful attempt to communicate with me was on Christmas Day when I was pregnant. I woke up before Gil and just lay there on the bed in our sunny room with my hands on my stomach. Suddenly I felt a little bump, a thump I hadn't felt before. I tapped twice, on the place where I'd felt you move; you thumped back at me. I stayed there for a long time in that same position, waiting to feel you again. It was my favorite thing about being pregnant and the thing I now miss the most, feeling that secret movement, feeling you nuzzle and twist, burrowing in and sliding across, a mystery unfolding inside me.

Wednesday, January 19

There are some things, perhaps, mothers shouldn't tell daughters. But I trust that you will be reading this as an adult and not as a child and therefore will be able to view what I say with some detachment, without automatically assuming blame or guilt or exacerbating any complex already induced by me. Perhaps you are reading this after the birth of your own child; perhaps you already know what I am about to say. Mothering is just so unending, so overwhelming, so draining, so immediate. Yesterday was a day where I had no time to do or think about anything that wasn't directly related to you. I spent four hours trying to get you to sleep, but you did not want to sleep in your crib, only on me. Hour after hour I would get you calm only to have you wake up screaming if I put you in your crib. This lasted until 3:00 A.M., when I was finally able to slide you into bed without you noticing. By that time I was a hysterical mess. I hated everything. I hated that you weren't going to bed at 7:30 like you usually do. I hated that I had to be the one to rock you, hour after hour. I hated that Gil seemed to imply that there should be nothing else I'd want to do more than give, give, give, scream after scream, hour after hour. I hated feeling robbed of my own needs. I hated sitting there in the dark, rocking myself into vertigo. I hated that all the plans I had for the evening were ruined, hated that I'd be too tired in the morning to run on the treadmill, hated that I still have fifteen pounds of pregnancy weight and that I have to run on the treadmill to lose it, hated it that none of my other mom friends had any trouble losing their weight, hated that I have to be the one with the inexhaustible resources, the never-ending patience, the constant love and understanding, the all-encompassing compassion. If there is anything that makes me not want to have another baby, it is this essential conflict, this hatred of being trapped in laundry, bottles, schedules, tiny runny noses. But none of this is about you: I don't wish you were never born, I don't resent you, I don't want to give you away. I just wish I could have a break longer than the hour or so that is your nap. I wish I could have my time back, my body back. I wish there was a better division of labor than Daddy when he has time and Mommy all day, all night.

And yet last night when I went to the movies while you played with Daddy, I missed you unbearably. I saw babies on the movie screen and all I could think of was your cheeks, your hands, your little butt as you try to crawl and move around. I couldn't wait to get home, I was sure something horrible had happened while I was away and I would return to find Gil answering questions from the police or climbing in the ambulance as they sped you off to the children's hospital. I came home to a dark, quiet house, 9:00 P.M., both you and Daddy asleep.

Friday, April 21

Things are really good these days. Even though you have abandoned your morning nap, you have gotten into a good routine, and I have really come to enjoy the rhythm of our days together. You are saying "bath" and "duck" now, and you are quite the explorer, into everything. Last night when I gave you a bath you were having so much fun, laughing with your duck, splashing in the water. . . . I soaped you up and rinsed you off and made you laugh by poking your juicy thighs and saying, "Juicy, juicy jellybean!" We had so much fun, but I was sad too. You are quickly becoming less of a baby and more of a toddler, less entirely mine, secret from the real world. One day you will be a secret from me, your inner life—your body—private, no more of the physical closeness we share now. All of these milestones you are reaching are both happy and sad occasions for me.

Tuesday, November 21

I went to see a movie the other day with your dad and was reminded again how motherhood has changed me. I can no longer watch, read, listen to, or think about anything without thinking of its connectedness to me and you. All I could think about watching this movie was you, how you might react in the situations I saw on screen, how I might react if something in the story happened to you. All I could think about were the unspeakable things human beings can do to one another, how terrified I am of your growing up and getting hurt or abused or slapped around by a guy or intimidated by a boss, or any of the millions of things that could happen.

But I know my real fear about your growing older is not only about the millions of things that could happen. It is about how afraid I am of what I imagine as the inevitable separation that will come between us. I don't know why I am so convinced it will happen, but I am afraid that it will, and I am already mourning the loss of these days when you had no choice but to love me.

• • •

Sunday, December 24

Two years ago tomorrow is the anniversary of the first time I felt you move inside me. You were private, you were only mine, and although I didn't truthfully imagine you were consciously trying to tell me something with your twists and kicks I did savor the fact that it was privileged communication. Just now I put you in your crib with your bunny and your bottle, stroked your hair, and told you I love you. Tomorrow you'll wake up and tell me all kinds of things, use your new words, gasp with delight when you tear the paper off yet more presents, and race around for all the world to see. You haven't been entirely mine for eighteen months now, and even back then, pre-world, I felt our separateness. But now the fact is heightened as you spend your five hours a week at playschool without me there, play with the baby-sitter all day Fridays without me there—become yourself without me there. Every once in a while, like now, when I am weepy and a little saddened by the holidays, I feel a pang when I think about these things, about your being in the world all by yourself. But I know that's entirely the point: you were born to be here, and now I must stand back and stand by for the treasured occasional hug and kiss.

III

Mother Tongue

—⟋⟍⟋⟍⟋—

Recovery. The crisis is resolved by a number of methods such that the person ends up learning the language and culture of the host country.

—Kalvero Oberg

Gradual Adjustment: The crisis is over and you are on your way to recovery. This step may come so gradually that, at first, you will be unaware it is happening. Once you begin to orient yourself and are able to interpret some of the subtle cultural clues and cues which passed by unnoticed earlier, the culture seems more familiar. You become more comfortable in it and feel less isolated from it. Gradually, too, your sense of humor returns and you realize the situation is not hopeless after all.

—The University of Iowa's Web site on culture shock

Birthing, raising my daughter through infancy to childhood, was a hard process of knowledge, a kind of physical endurance for us both, bearing knowledge of survival; of the simplest facts of eating, sleeping, and the struggle to exist. All around me floated archetypal mothers, . . . young, carefree-looking women running in slow motion across fields, swooping to caress angelic children, unbearably lithe models grinning over clean babies in clean blankets. I could not see through them. My own experience waited blind and dumb, unspoken. —Susan Griffin

It is hard to speak about mothering. Overwhelmed with greeting-card sentiment, we have no realistic language in which to capture the ordinary/ extraordinary pleasures and pains of maternal work.

—Sara Ruddick

Wednesdays in the Park

We meet every Wednesday, in the park, until the summer cools to fall and then freezes into winter and the trees no longer have leaves to shade us. The pregnant women with their maternity-clothed bellies walk by us longingly, expectantly, watching us for a glimpse into their future. We are all on the other side, past the wondering and waiting, past the imagining, past the unknowable. The mothers with the double strollers walk by us longingly too, but their longing is for a time when it was easier, when there was only one baby to figure out, one child to soothe. Every week we meet in the park with our babies and talk about how much they have grown, what new things they are doing, how little sleep we have gotten. I do not think our time right now is easy, and I cannot imagine the energy it would take to deal with more than one child. But we do not always talk about the difficulties.

I worried about mothering, the way even the word is freighted with responsibility, when I was pregnant, but it was more abstract: I worried about the concept, the metaphor, the theory of it, and I am glad I did, for even now I think about these things. But back then I was buoyed by the innateness of pregnancy, by the fact that being pregnant made me a mother without actually having to mother anyone. Being a mother with a baby out in the world is not so innate, at least not for me. Now I am both metaphor and reality, theory and fact, and I see the way young, childless women look at me on the street.

I loved being pregnant, but I was ambivalent about motherhood. I worried that I wouldn't know what to do, that I would do something horribly wrong. I worried that I would birth out my normal self along with the baby, that I'd transform into my mother, suddenly sprouting curlers and Dr. Scholl's, suddenly carrying an immense purse filled with everything from cough drops to underwear, suddenly eating an entire bunch of grapes on the way to the checkout counter at the supermarket and throwing down the empty stalk to be weighed. I worried motherhood would be a transition that would forever separate me from my former self. I wanted desperately to connect with other people who were making that transition, who might reassure me that I really was still me despite the enormous changes in my body, in my life.

After my daughter was born I meandered with her through the park, wrestling with a bulky stroller I did not yet know how to steer, too afraid of tripping and falling to subject her to being carried snugly against me in a Baby Björn. We traveled paths and walkways I'd had neither the leisure nor inclination to walk before, every crack in the sidewalk an affront to my new stroller's stubborn wheels. I'd been told to come here, to wander around Rittenhouse Square with my newborn, because in our city this place is some sort of baby mecca. Surely here I would meet someone else similarly shell-shocked to be pushing a pram, surely here I'd meet another new mother feeling otherworldly and awkward toting around all the equipment necessary to care for a tiny new life. I looked for women like me, women who might feel vaguely impostor-like in their postpartum costumes of diaper backpacks and nursing wear, who might feel as though they were merely acting the part of the mom, who might feel as though any minute the actual, self-assured real parents of the newborn they were pushing around would rush up and rightfully take their darling child home with them, where she belonged.

In the park I saw mothers at home in their motherhood, casually talking with one another and only peripherally watching their toddlers play and climb on the benches. I saw women walking purposefully through the square holding hands with their eight-year-olds, their ten-year-olds. I saw women standing watch while their five-year-olds attempted to ride their first bikes. And finally I saw a woman like me, disheveled, bleary-eyed, pushing a stroller that faced toward her instead of out to the world the way it would for an older child. We gravitated toward one another as though we were magnetized, and I discovered that having a baby with you is one of the best conversational ice-breakers there can be.

Walking around by myself I would never have approached another person and struck up a conversation just because they appeared to be friendly. But with a baby, the rules of social engagement completely change. As soon as we came near each other, we smiled, both of us craning to peek in the other's stroller, both of us asking, "How old?" Both of us desperate for a connection.

As it turned out, this woman's baby was just a day younger than mine. We had been pregnant, labored, and delivered in this small town of a city, and yet we had never met until that day in the park. We talked for nearly an hour, until our babies awoke and we were surprised into remembering that we had to respond. Before we left, we agreed to meet again, in the park, where all the mothers seemed to be. "We can start our own playgroup!" she said enthusiastically, trying out one of the new vocabulary words of our new vocation. We were both excited by the idea despite the fact that technically our babies would not be playing with each other, but rather sleeping in their strollers while we talked. We were both just excited to be *doing* something, accomplishing a normal, nonmaternal task like making adult social plans—something we both used to do and found unremarkable before our world suddenly revolved around our infants' schedules. We agreed to get together the next Wednesday, an eternity of sleepless nights and blurry days from our first meeting, and we both returned to our solitary existence of scaling the learning curve of new motherhood.

Our Wednesday meetings started out small, just the two of us with our newborns. Then another new mom would walk by and ask if she could join us. Then another new mom would find us, and another, and another. We were all hungry for companionship, hungry to talk about our experiences with pregnancy, with labor and delivery, with this strange new life of motherhood. We were so elated to find other people who understood—in a way that even our husbands and certainly our childless friends could not—what we were dealing with day to day, what we had been initiated into. Gradually our group grew to fifteen or so new moms, and it became a regular thing, our Wednesday meeting. We had found each other.

What I really wanted to talk about with other new moms were the things I didn't hear anyone really talking about. I wanted to know if mothering was difficult for them too, whether everyone else had the same doubts or if it was challenging only for me. But it has proved difficult to ask about those things openly. We talk about our babies' physical progress, how they are beginning to roll or starting to raise their heads. We talk about losing pregnancy weight. We talk about feeding and diapering. I am so hungry for contact with people who understand the daily routine of life with a new baby that this almost suffices.

Eventually I discover one or two women in the group who linger afterward and talk about the more profound difficulties of adjusting to motherhood. We talk in hushed voices about postpartum depression, about hating our spouses in the middle of the night, about our frightening wishes to just run away and be normal, non-mom people again. We confess our fears quickly, blinking back tears of frustration, and say our goodbyes until next week. One day, in the midst of one of these conversations, a pregnant woman approaches us. She looks radiant, glowing in accordance with the cliché of how a pregnant woman should look. She is nine months pregnant, she tells us. She's looking for a mom's group to join once the baby's born. We tell her about our Wednesday meetings and invite her to come sometime. She looks so relieved, and we tell her we understand, we tell her how great it is to have the support of other new moms. Then she asks, "So, what's it like?" And we stare blankly. "What's it like being a mom?" she asks. One of my friends whispers to me, "Should we really tell her?" and we look at one another, silently deciding whether or not to burst the woman's beautiful, hopeful pregnant bubble. "It's great," someone finally says. "It's hard, and you don't get a lot of sleep, but it's great."

What else can you say, really? No one knows what it's like until they are there, and so often no one is really ready to hear the gritty answers to the question, anyway. She wanted reassurance, a postcard from life on the other side saying, "Everything's wonderful! Wish you were here!" That's what all of us want, really, and that's why we show up each

Wednesday, whether or not we talk about the reality of what we're experiencing in all its painful complexity.

Each Wednesday I am reminded of the normalcy of what I am doing from day to day. Mothering in the isolation of my house seems so often like a superhuman task, so alienating, so spectacular, so solitary. But meeting with the other mothers every week reminds me of the absolute ordinariness of motherhood, the reassuring mundaneness of what I do on a daily basis, the sheer handleability of it all. Every one of us does it. I can too. We do not really talk about feeling helpless, we do not really talk about feeling lost; yet I cannot tell you how much I look forward to those Wednesday meetings, where we are all bound together, no matter what we talk about, by our motherhood.

Confessions of a Bottle Feeder

Here's how pro-breast-feeding I was: when my daughter was born, I hadn't even purchased a bottle, I hadn't even purchased a pump. I would be at home, I would not need to be pumping, that's the kind of breast-feeding mom I was going to be. Sure, I had taken a breast-feeding class and talked about my concerns that it might not work, that there might be complications, but I hadn't seriously thought anything would go wrong.

Here's the reality: fair-skinned and flat-nippled, with a baby who would neither latch nor suck (not that she could find anything to latch onto), my breasts so sensitive after delivery that the breast shells I used tore off my skin when I removed them, the pump a cross between a vacuum cleaner and an angry porcupine, the pain of attempting to pump worse than actually giving birth. And here's how it ended: with the lactation consultant staring me straight in the eye and telling me, "Feed your baby. Formula is not the end of the world."

I remember being four months pregnant and visiting with a friend who had a small baby. My friend told me a cautionary tale, the moral of which was: in case the breast-feeding doesn't work out, don't worry, it doesn't mean you're a bad person. She told me her story, how she tried for a month, stuck it out despite the pain and her baby's screaming and weight loss. The point of it was that her pediatrician finally told her the objective was a healthy, happy family unit, not a dehydrated baby and a resentful, guilty mom. But I tuned it out. I know I smiled and nodded my head appropriately, but I remember thinking to myself, "That's nice, but it's going to work for me." We were on opposite sides of that gulf between the newly pregnant and the newly delivered, and my side was the one characterized by blissful ignorance. I saw the issue the way it was presented to me in everything I read about breast-feeding versus formula feeding: it was black and white, good mom or bad mom. But being unable to breast-feed my baby led me into a world of gray.

Successful breast-feeders might find fault with my lactation consultant, they might say she let me down by encouraging me to go with formula when it became clear that breast-feeding was not working for us. Militant breast-feeders might say it was a matter of will, a matter of morality: I could have done it and I should have done it, and the fact that I ended my suffering prematurely is an indication of my maternal deficiencies. I don't mind that avid breast-feeders have an opinion about formula, but I do mind that they cast judgment on women like me, women who have chosen formula, without experiencing the debate from my perspective.

Wielding a bottle these days is tantamount to hitting your kid in the supermarket. I have had women in the park confront me to inquire as to whether I was feeding my baby a bottle of breast milk or formula; I have seen the looks of other mothers as I, the lone formula-feeder, mixed my baby's bottle. In a heated discussion on an Internet bulletin board, a woman I've never met told me I should consider something she called relactation, since according to her if I was feeding my baby formula, I might as well be giving her dog food. I wanted to respond that I, of course, feed my baby only the finest *cat* food and not only does it give her coat a nice glossy sheen, it also brings out the "frisky" in her. And as for relactation, that makes about as much sense to me as telling a woman who delivered by C-section to stuff that six- or eight- or ten-month-old baby back in there and do it the "right" way this time. But what I really wanted to know is why was she so invested in my choice? I'm not uneducated, I'm not uninformed; I am a reasonably intelligent human being making the best decision I can after much thought, research, and heartache. I am not out to convince everyone to do things my way. Why should everyone care that I do things theirs?

I don't see parents who smoke being attacked with the same intensity as those who formula-feed despite the fact that the effects of secondhand smoke are far more serious than those of a year of formula. I don't see mothers who scream at their kids in public being lectured on proper parenting techniques despite the fact that emotional abuse is far more stunting than not breast-feeding. I don't see the parents who feed their kids supersize meals at McDonald's being pulled aside for a crash course in toddler nutrition. And yet that is what it is like in the breast-feeding crusade: those of us who don't breast-feed, for whatever reason, or decide to stop, for whatever reason, are scolded like children, considered ignorant and dangerous, reviled on the many Web sites devoted to breast-feeding.

And that's another question I have: is this "breast is best" mentality about breast milk or breast-feeding? What about the mom who pumps? What about the mom who breast-feeds for only ten weeks or six months? Are those women worse mothers than the mom who breast-feeds for a year, two years? There seems to be a not-so-subtle hierarchy in the breast-feeding worldview, with the exclusively breast-feeding at the top, the half-pumping/half-breast-feeding moms somewhere after that, the exclusive pumpers even farther down the line, and of course at the bottom, those lowly formula-feeders.

What I'm interested in is the middle ground—somewhere between the stereotypes, between the family-bed/homeschool/cloth-diaper militancy of the avid breast-feeders and the ignorance of the uninformed bottle feeder must be a place where women can choose to fortify their babies without their particular method determining their fitness as a mother.

The fact is we are all terrified (or should be) about becoming parents. Will we do it right? What if the desperate thoughts we have in the middle of the night when our baby won't stop screaming, or on those days when our wilding toddler is really getting on that last nerve, mean we're bad parents, bad people? I know that part of my determination to breast-feed was because I thought it would make me the Good Mother, that my obvious motherly devotion and effort would stamp out any bad-mom potential lurking in me.

It is much easier to demonize something outside of ourselves than to face what frightens us, so breast-feeding becomes the talisman against our fears. We think: breast-feeding will save me from making the mistakes my mother made; breast-feeding will make my child smarter; breast-feeding will make my child immune to allergies, to sickness, to heartache, to danger, to death. We all want to provide the absolute best life for our child, but the fact is that so much more than breast-feeding determines the quality of life. Say you breast-feed. Say you breast-feed for a year, even for two years. What then? Won't your child still have to face the world, go to school, grow up, become a teenager, get his or her heart broken, be rejected by or accepted to the college she aspires to attend, have a career and a life that may or may not bring him happiness or dissatisfaction? Won't the world intervene anyway?

I'm not advocating feeding your baby formula because the world is a cruel, random place so what does it matter. I'm just saying, formula is not the end of the world.

And if you think that's a bunch of dog food, that's fine by me.

A Fine Mess

Oh, this is just great.

I was just starting to get over my guilt about not having a spotless house, when I came across this headline from the *Washington Post*: "Straighten Up Your Room: A Study Finds That Kids Who Live in Tidy Homes Are Likely to Clean Up Financially."

This explains a few things about me, for sure, and why I'm not raking in the bucks, but I was dismayed to read about what the current state of my home implies for my daughter's future. My philosophy, as of late, has been that a clean house is pretty much the sign of a serious mental illness, and that as long as the Tylenol and the cat food are inaccessible to my daughter, our apartment has the Good Housekeeping Seal of Approval. But after reading this article I'm not so sure.

"Kids from cleaner homes make more money and attain higher educational levels than their grubby-living counterparts," the author stated unequivocally. Does my home qualify as grubby? Let's see: there are dishes piled up in the sink. From my bedroom I can smell the ripe stench of the Diaper

Genie. There's rice in the carpet. The living room is currently overtaken by a giant tent, beneath which many Honey Nut Cheerios have been crushed by toys that have never been disinfected with antibacterial wipes. My husband uses our dining room table as a horizontal filing cabinet and the desk in our room as a hamper. "Grubby living" may be putting it nicely.

Sure, I've been feeling pangs of guilt about my less-than-stellar housekeeping skills. To make myself feel better, I've stayed away from other moms' discussions about how often they iron, change the sheets, make the bed, and do laundry, since my answers are "never," "when I have to," "if someone's coming over," and "when the dirty-clothes pile is as tall as I am." I've resigned myself to being satisfied with having time only to make a dent in the layer of dust that seems to fall over the house the minute I Swiffer it up. I've made a deal with myself that if I can't actually fold the laundry and put it away in its rightful place, I can at least take it out of the dryer, and I do pick up the toys each night just to give the illusion that the house is not overrun with clutter. I have faced the fact that there are only so many hours in a day, and I almost completely accept (for I still guiltily flinch every time I see that Martha Stewart commercial where she's half naked and admonishes me to change those bedsheets "every day!") that, without a maid, deep cleaning is just not a priority. Heck, between working at home, cooking, paying the bills, answering phone calls and e-mails—

oh, and caring for my daughter—I'm lucky if I *get* into the shower once a week, let alone clean it.

So my apartment is not the apartment of a mom with a cleaning person, and it's not the apartment of a mom with an obsessive-compulsive hatred of germs. But it's also not the apartment of the old lady you see on the news, with fifty cats and garbage coming out of her windows because she can't bring herself to throw anything away. On the cleanliness continuum, I'm guessing my grubby-living quotient is about average. It's a fine mess: my daughter wears clean clothes and doesn't usually leave the house covered in Magic Marker. You can walk around most of the place without having to kick things out of the way. We do take the garbage out eventually.

I thought that was acceptable, but according to the *Washington Post* article, it might not be. Researchers at Northwestern University, Columbia University, and the University of Michigan found that of kids from homes ranging from "dirty" to "so-so" to "clean" to "very clean," "those who grew up in homes that were at least 'clean' went on to finish 13.6 years of school. Typically, men and women from 'not very clean' homes only finished high school. [And] offspring from neater abodes earned . . . about $3,100 more annually."

This brought to mind a few things: first, who funded this study? Martha Stewart? The makers of Lysol? And second, I'd better start teaching my daughter how to say "Would you like fries with that?"

• • •

Perhaps the authors of the study intended to show that environment can positively affect children's potential, and perhaps they meant to give sloppy moms like me a kick in the pants to drag out the vacuum cleaner and whip out that toilet brush. But what it conjures up for me is that outdated, perfectly coifed vision of mom in a poofy dress and frilly apron: get those sinks gleaming and get dinner on the table! Take pride in your housewifely duties—your children's future is at stake! Because make no mistake about it, this study is not directed at fathers, who are not mentioned at all aside from their pre-parent incarnations as boys who might be adversely affected by their mothers' untidiness. What's next, the study that shows that children fare better if they have moms who bring home the bacon, fry it up in a pan, and never let dad forget he's a man?

But on the plus side, those statistics mean that I'm a grubby-living overachiever: I grew up in a decidedly "so-so" house, yet I finished eighteen, count 'em, eighteen years of school. Of course, with my so-so, grubby-living background, I don't make all that much money, and six of those school years involved student loans I will be paying back well into my retirement. But my mate may even things out: my husband grew up in what I'm sure my mother-in-law would call a "very clean" house and has more earning potential than I do. So maybe this means there's hope for my daughter after all.

I wasn't always like this, chasing after dust bunnies that shouldn't have been allowed to gather in the first place. I used to be fastidious and tidy. But that was back when I had time. It's taken a huge adjustment for me to go from control-freak pre-parent to letting-things-slide-a-little mommy, and I'm sure I'm not the only mother who wonders if the small things I do or don't do will somehow impact my child in ways I can't imagine. So a study like this one just preys on my fears. It just feeds the doubt.

My only solace in all this is a small paragraph discreetly tucked into the middle of the piece: if you go overboard in your quest for cleanliness, it cautions, the benefits of clean living for your children "get sucked up with the dirt" you're frantically vacuuming away. And then, on a more ominous note: "The highest level of cleanliness is associated with the lowest level of attainment later." So I guess you really can have too much of a good thing.

Did you hear that, Martha?

Sleeping Like a Baby

Whoever came up with the phrase "sleeping like a baby" either never had a baby or meant it ironically. Any new parent can attest to the fact that no baby sleeps as contentedly as that cliché implies (except for when you go to have her picture taken, or visit your best friend who's never seen the baby before, or at any other time you'd rather have the kid awake). Sleep is a constant topic among new moms, and how much or how little your baby sleeps often becomes yet another barometer of maternal success or failure.

Granted, in the first few weeks and months, there's not that much else to talk about besides how much they weigh, how much they weighed when they were born, and how much they sleep. It's not like they're hitting any major milestones other than adjusting to life outside of that nine-month bed and breakfast they used to call home. And besides, it's always nice to commiserate. So it's natural, in a way, for new moms to question each other on the topic of sleep, because usually no one's getting any.

I was lucky, although I didn't realize it until later: I had a bona fide good sleeper on my hands. Sure, I felt sleep-deprived, and sure, we had our nights of pacing the floor at 1:00 A.M., 3:30 A.M. and 5:00 A.M., watching the late-late-late-late movie. But compared to what I heard from other moms, I had it easy. At two weeks, my daughter was basically sleeping through the night. She might wake up for a snack somewhere in the middle, but we could usually count on at least ten hours of sleeping, most of those hours being consecutive. I quickly learned not to discuss this with my new-mom friends, most of whom were subjects in an ongoing sleep-deprivation experiment, at the mercy of their babies' every-hour-on-the-hour wake-up calls. What tipped me off, besides the bug-eyed looks I'd get when I'd admit my baby slept five hours at a stretch, was a line from our pediatrician at my daughter's two-month appointment. "How is she sleeping?" the doctor asked. "Pretty good," I said, not knowing any better. "She sleeps about ten hours a night." The pediatrician laughed out loud. "If I were you," she told me and my husband, "I'd get down on my knees and thank whatever god you believe in, because, believe you me, that is a gift from above!" We felt a little smug after that, sure that our baby's good sleeping habits had something to do with our doing something right.

I pretty much stayed out of other moms' discussions about sleep-deprivation, feeling I had no right chiming in when I was probably the most well rested of all of them, but I heard the names of baby sleep gurus tossed around and debated hotly. The way I understood it, the current purveyors of sleep psychology were your basic Democrats and Republicans. On the liberal Democratic side you had your attachment-parenting, family-bed-encouraging Dr. William Sears and, more conservative, your a-little-crying-never-hurt advocate, Dr. Ferber. On the Republican side of the debate there was Dr. Weissbluth (who, a friend confided, was referred to as "the nap Nazi" by his colleagues at Northwestern University Hospital, since his theories about good sleeping involve stringent rules about where and when babies should nap) and the abhorrent Gary Ezzo, author of the controversial *Babywise*.

I listened to everyone's experiences with the various techniques, from moms delighted with the family bed to moms who let their babies "cry it out," from moms who followed a rigid schedule with their infants to moms who didn't care where their babies slept so long as they actually slept. I heard all kinds of stories from the trenches—heartbreaking stories of sleep deprivation and helplessness, moms and dads crying along with their babies, and funny stories about the lengths we'll go to to get our babies to sleep. Nearly everyone who was trying to get their baby to sleep in the crib experienced the "butt phenomenon," where the baby, after falling asleep in mom or dad's arms, would jolt awake screaming as soon as its little butt touched the crib mattress. Everyone had experienced the tension of finally getting the baby to sleep and then having to steal out of the room like a ninja, hoping against hope that the squeak of a floorboard or the sound of the door closing quietly would go unnoticed. One mom told of a friend who was at her wit's end trying to get her baby to sleep: she had tried everything and finally discovered that her baby would fall asleep comfortably only if mom or dad was in the room with her, so the parents took turns sleeping on the floor of the baby's room. Eventually they tried to ease out of the habit, each night sleeping a little closer to the door, until finally they slept just outside the door, with the door open so the baby could see them. Then they slept on the floor with just their legs showing through the doorway. Then just their feet showing. Then finally they just left their shoes there. It was pretty hilarious in the telling, and I think just about everyone listening related to the desperate measures. Sleep is something you don't want to mess with.

Our sleep problems began just as my friends' babies were getting the hang of what's supposed to happen at night. At eight months or so, our normally easy-sleeping daughter suddenly refused to sleep unless she was in my arms. Sometimes I could trick her into falling asleep by dancing around the room with her on my shoulder, but inevitably as soon as she realized she was drooling on her crib mattress instead of me, she'd wake up screaming. Hour after hour, it seemed, we'd dance in the darkness of her room. Sometimes I'd just walk to the rhythm of what we were listening to (Paul Simon's *Rhythm of the Saints*, a CD permanently burned into my cerebral cortex); sometimes I'd invent choreography; sometimes I'd use it as an excuse to exercise, doing squats and lunging in time to the beat. But no matter how long we danced or what style I danced in, the scenario always seemed to end with her waking up as soon as I put her down.

After nights and nights of this, I was at my wit's end. My friends offered advice based on all the techniques they'd tried months before, back when our babies were supposed to be learning how to sleep. Desperate, I tried nearly everything they suggested. We tried letting her sleep with us, but evidently our bed was a giant playpen, and merely setting her on it triggered waves of alertness and excitement that accomplished nothing even remotely resembling drowsiness, let alone actual sleep. We tried a modified Ferber method, letting her cry for a few minutes at a time and quickly going back in to soothe her. This failed miserably in our first attempt: she cried so hard for those interminable five minutes that she threw up. The guilt of that alone would have been enough to put an end to our foray into Ferber territory, but in addition to that, by the time she was comforted and calmed down, the crib cleaned, the carpet sprayed, and new bedsheets located, she was wide awake and ready for playtime. We, of course, were not. We tried pushing her in the stroller, hypnotizing her in the swing, everything short of giving up our primo parking space and driving her around. One night, desperate, I even climbed in the crib with her, thinking that if she wanted me that badly I'd just sleep in there. (This, too, backfired—though my husband got a kick out of it.)

It was unbelievable to me that I was suddenly on the other side of the "good sleeping baby equals good mommy" equation. What was I doing wrong? Was her reluctance to sleep a damning indictment of my maternal shortcomings? I began to change the subject when the topic of baby sleep came up in conversation with other moms. I began to smoothe over the truth a little, claiming minute progress on the sleep front when in fact there was none. I began to outright lie. Yes, of course she sleeps through the night! Maternal stamp of approval earned. End of discussion.

Gradually, we moved through our sleepless nights. I began to realize that what comforted my daughter was being reassured that I was close by, so through night after sleep-deprived night of trial and error, I hit upon a technique that worked for all of us. It was a combination of rocking her to sleep, putting her to bed, and responding immediately when she cried, something frowned upon in the books. But eventually our good sleeper was back, content to drift off knowing I'd be there right away if she needed me. Had I somehow improved as a mother between the time that she stopped sleeping and the time she started up again? No—in fact, if anything, my maternal skills had probably deteriorated, thanks to months of sleep-deprivation. Her renewed interest in slumber probably had more to do with the fact that with babies and young children, no pattern stays constant for too long. But it took that humbling experience to fully understand that a baby's sleeping or not sleeping really, truly, one hundred percent has nothing to do with the quality of a person's parenting. As much as I realized that intellectually, I had still, in my daughter's heyday of good sleeping, relied on her soporific prodigality as being proof of my inherent skill, proof of the fact that I was doing a good job. Now I recognize it for what it was: a fluke.

As my daughter got older, I realized she wasn't a sleeper at heart, her early track record notwithstanding. She gave up her morning nap shortly after she started walking, at nine months. And over a year later, the summer she turned two, she phased out her afternoon naps as well. She now clocks in roughly twelve hours of sleep a day, usually all of that at night. If she happens to be seduced into napping by a drive in the car or a long walk in the stroller on a hot, sleep-inducing day, she will stay up later than usual, going to sleep at a time that her body somehow reckons with a complex formula that ends up granting her a total of her usual twelve hours.

Of course, things are also different now: now she sleeps in our bed with us—something that to most people represents a huge regression in our sleep "training." But what I have discovered in my adventures in baby and toddler sleep is that the most crucial part of the equation is how much sleep we are getting, not where we are getting it. My daughter has slept inside me, beside me, in a sling, in a stroller, in a crib in the next room, in a "big-girl bed" and nestled next to me in my bed, and each of these places has had its own time and place in her life of slumber.

The sleeping arrangement that works best for us is the one that enables me to get as much sleep as possible, because a rested mama is a happy mama—and a happy mama is a better mama than an exhausted, anxious, sleep-deprived wreck of a mama. Right now that arrangement is having "bed-night," as Emi calls it, in our king-size bed, all of us together. When that stops affording us a good night's sleep, we'll move on to something else that works better. For now, though, we pile into the bed together, read stories and tell stories and snuggle together, and eventually drift off together, sleeping like babies until the morning comes.

I'm an Idiot

I am an idiot.

Sometimes I forget I am not a normal adult person, free to make my own schedule and determine the trajectory of my days. Sometimes, especially when my daughter takes a rare afternoon-long nap, and I am absorbed in my work, I forget that there was a time when working uninterrupted was actually *not* something I fantasized about. Sometimes I even imagine that I can be a mother and still be a fully functional, autonomous human being. But then I do something idiotic, and I am reminded that, for now at least, those two things are mutually exclusive.

Let me back up: I work from home, part-time. This means different things to different people. To those people who deal with a commute, office politics, and bureaucratic headaches, it means my life is one big nonstop party with an average workday consisting of a few phone calls while I lounge in my pajamas watching soaps, *Oprah*, and Lifetime midday movies. To people who work from home, the meaning is more clear: I "work" from "home," meaning my job and my domicile are in the same place at the same time, defying a crucial law of physics. These people understand how difficult it can be to be taken seriously on the work front ("But you're at home! Part-time!!"), and how impossible it can sometimes be to get anything done on the home front ("What do you mean, you have to work? Can't you just do this errand for me?"). To the other moms who work from home, the meaning is obvious: I get absolutely nothing done.

Since I work from home, every day is take-your-daughter-to-work day. My eighteen-month-old daughter Emi does go to playschool two mornings a week for a few hours, and we did finally arrange for a baby-sitter to come on Fridays for the whole day, but the rest of the time— weekends, afternoons, nights, holidays, sick days, deadline days—it's the twenty-four-hour-mommy show, all mommy, all the time. But you might imagine that in the year and a half I've had to get used to juggling my mama duties and my worker duties, I've had ample time to learn how to strike a balance, right? Ha. Let me share with you the story of my day today and you can see what happens when I become overconfident in my abilities to handle the merging of two worlds.

My day starts at 6:00 A.M. because Emi's up for some reason. It's a school day, though, so it's okay, I can deal: just two and a half hours till we're out the door. So after I get back from dropping her off at school I get a call on my work line and it's the editor in chief of the magazine I work for. He says, "Oh, by the way, a whole bunch of us are in town today for a meeting, and we thought we could see you for lunch!"

I've known that they were coming to town for weeks, but only because I found out through a client, since everyone higher up always forgets I'm here (did I mention I work from home? Part-time?). I had called my boss last week to ask her if I should be offended that no one had officially mentioned the visit to me and she said to just count myself lucky until they remember that I exist. So I pretend that this is the first I've heard of this. I tell him lunch would be great, but I don't have a baby-sitter, so I can't go.

But he says, "No, it'll be perfect—we're not lunching with clients, it's just us. Just bring the baby to the restaurant, we'd love to see her!"

I agree, because I'm an idiot.

So I pack up all kinds of food, toys, and other distractions, and pick up Emi from school. We go to this super-fancy restaurant (Did I mention this lunch was taking place at one of the nicest restaurants in Philadelphia? Did I mention that I'm an idiot?) just in time for Emi's lunchtime/naptime meltdown, and stressful episodes ensue. Here's a sampling of today's hilarity:

EMI: [screaming]
MAGAZINE BIGWIG #1: Oh, Andi, I'd like you to meet Wayne.
EMI: [screaming]

ANDI: Hi, Wayne, sorry about the noise. Nice to meet you.

EMI: NO!!! DOWN!!! GO AWAY!!! NO!!! DON'T!!! BYE-BYE!!! GO AWAY!!! NO!!!!!!

ANDI: This is Emi . . . can you tell she's almost two?

MAGAZINE BIGWIG #2 (WAYNE): [unintelligible over the screaming]

ANDI: I'm sorry—Wayne, was it?—I didn't catch your title. What do you do here?

WAYNE: Uh . . . I'm the NEW PUBLISHER.

– Curtain –

I should add that after this there was general freaking out and ketchup-flinging on Emi's part and near tears on mine as I was hit in the head by a flying cell phone during part of said freaking. Everyone at the lunch did a good job of pretending to ignore the huge pile of goldfish, peas, and spaghetti on Emi's side of the table and were solicitous about helping us try to remove the ketchup stains from the fancy tablecloth using baby wipes. Several otherwise non-baby types even engaged in attempts at peekaboo. But I sensed that perhaps this was not the scene anyone had envisioned when planning to attend a business lunch. Emi and I excused ourselves and left as soon as I had finished as much of my lunch as was possible to finish while trying to talk business as if the ketchup-covered toddler throwing a tantrum in my lap wasn't there (Did I mention that she abandoned her "big-girl chair" booster seat about fifteen minutes into this two-hour lunch?).

But my day did not end there: after we returned home from lunch, Emi did not take a nap, so I couldn't answer e-mails, do the editorial work waiting for me with deadlines looming, or return people's calls. Work from home? Not likely. After a final, total meltdown—screaming, crying, you name it—Emi fell asleep for the night at about 5:30. So I expect to be up at the crack of dawn tomorrow, if not several times tonight. And now that she's finally asleep, my day is just beginning.

And that was my feeble attempt at being a normal adult person, going to a restaurant for a business lunch. Let it be a lesson to us all.

What's in a Name?

My daughter has my last name. No, I am not single. No, I'm not separated or divorced. No, she wasn't conceived with the assistance of mail-order sperm and a lab tech. I am by all accounts a conventional person in a conventional marriage. My daughter has my last name because of the simple if unconventional fact that my husband and I decided to give it to her.

Truthfully, it was more my idea than his, at the beginning. I had kept my last name when we got married, and the idea that our child should receive his last name purely by default seemed rather arbitrary to me. Why should she have his last name? Why shouldn't she have mine? Either way—whether she had my name or his—one of the three of us would have a different last name, and we'd have some explaining to do. Why should I have to tell her that her name is different from mine because that's simply how people do it, how it's practically always been done?

"But how will people know she's mine?" my husband asked when I floated the idea.

"If she has *your* last name, how will people know she's *mine*?" I countered.

"Well, you'll be with her all the time," he said lamely.

"All the more reason for her to have my name," I shot back.

It was amazing how intertwined the concept of naming and ownership seemed to be. Both of us professed to be above the idea of possession—what a ridiculous notion, as if you could own someone—and yet as soon as the subject was broached, that's what rose to the surface. We revisited the topic off and on while I was pregnant, my husband managing to concede that if we were to decide purely on the criteria of what sounded nicer, my name would win, but refusing to fully capitulate and abandon the idea of his name being a part of hers.

After witnessing the birth of our daughter, my husband finally came to a decision. "That was the hardest thing I've ever seen anyone do," he told me. "I just stood here and gave you ice chips. She deserves your name." I'd heard about friends' husbands giving them gifts when their children were born, a bracelet or a necklace, but this was more meaningful than any piece of jewelry. We embraced our newborn and each other in the delivery room, ecstatic and teary and exhausted. "Did you hear that, Emily?" Gil asked her. "You have your mommy's last name."

When we arrived home from the hospital, my husband's

parents came to help. Hungry for any and all details about the birth and our hospital stay, they pored over the bags of literature, baby magazines, and how-to articles the staff had given us before sending us on our way. When they came to the hospital forms, they read aloud, "Emily Clare . . . *Buchanan?* Oh, look at that. They must have made a mistake!" Realizing we had committed the grave error of not discussing our decision with them first, I told them as calmly as I could manage, "Actually, it's not a mistake. Emily has my last name." There was a pause and then they said, "Oh. Okay." They were careful not to look at each other. Later, after they left, my husband said, "Wow, they took it pretty well, don't you think?" I shook my head and asked him, "Are you completely insane?"

Sure enough, within the hour they called to express how much our decision "hurt" them. Their hurt feelings stemmed from two things, really: one, that their first grandchild would not be carrying their last name, and two, that we had never discussed the subject with them before making our decision. I think it might have been thing number two that hurt more.

My husband talked on the phone with them for over an hour, trying to wrestle with the logic of their outdated reasoning: they firmly believed that a child should have the father's last name, that the husband's family name should be passed on to the next generation—and they also admitted to believing that a woman really should take her husband's last name when she marries. When confronted with the fact that given that belief, even if Emily did have their last name, it would be given up once she got married—and confronted in addition with the question of why it should be their family name rather than my family name that must be transferred to the next generation—they were silent. It was clearly more than the upsetting of tradition that was troubling to them.

They ended up asking the same question Gil had when the two of us had first discussed the issue: "But how will people know she's ours?" This time Gil had the answers. Because people won't be able to tell by looking at her that she doesn't share your last name. Because she shares your genes. Because you are her grandparents. Because she'll love you.

Gil tried to explain to them that our intent was not to hurt them or reject them or offend them in any way. He tried to explain that he thought of giving our daughter my last name as a way to honor both of us. But they didn't understand. How could it be an honor, how could it be supportive, how could it be such a good thing when none of their friends' children had done it, when they themselves felt so hurt? We both apologized to them for assuming that this first big decision about our daughter was ours alone to make. We apologized for not talking with them about it first. Finally, after more than an hour on the phone, we compromised: if they truly felt that uncomfortable with our decision, they could refer to Emily however they wanted; if it was so embarrassing, they didn't have to tell their friends their first and only granddaughter did not sport their last name. My husband told them, it doesn't matter what you call her. She's still your granddaughter, she's still our baby. It's just a name. Still, I don't think they finally felt relieved until we promised that our next child, if we had one, would have theirs.

When Gil and I first got married we talked about picking a new name that we'd both change to, but that proved difficult. Nowhere did our family trees intertwine, not even hundreds of years ago, so we had no names in common from which to choose. And the only one we even remotely liked was both too WASPy and too far down the alphabet. We spoke even more briefly about my husband's taking my last name, but despite the fact that my last name made him sound like a soap opera character or movie star, he just couldn't bring himself to do it. (Plus his parents objected—my last name reminds them of Pat Buchanan, to whom I am thankfully not related.)

It's not that his last name is so hideous—though it's definitely not one I'd ever pick if I had a choice—but it's long and unusual, and though it weeds out the telemarketers, some of whom give up after attempting to pronounce it, a lifetime of spelling it out over the phone made us think twice about saddling a defenseless newborn with it. And truth be told, even his parents considered shortening it to something more palatable when they emigrated from Israel in the mid-'60s. But whether because of sheer inertia or unresolvable reluctance, they never did.

My family has its own emotional reaction to the naming convention in general. I remember talking with my dad when I was in high school about the tradition of women giving up their names when they get married, and being surprised at his take on it. "Why should you have to give up your name?" he asked me. "Why should a woman have to abandon her identity? It's been your name your whole life, why not just keep it?" At the time, this was something I hadn't ever considered. Yet it made absolute sense. I decided if I ever got married, I would definitely keep my name.

My mother, though, is more Republican in her views on the topic. Despite her breezy attitude toward most other things in life, on the subject of names and naming she is surprisingly traditional. To this day, if she sends me a letter in the mail it will be addressed to "Andi Binenbaum"—or, barely capitulating to the reality that I am not my husband's last name—"Andi Buchanan Binenbaum." Though she and I never had the kind of emotional, extended conversation about my daughter's last name that Gil and I did with his parents, I can tell it was just as difficult for her to accept our flouting of tradition, to wrap her mind around the fact that her granddaughter has her last name (or, I should say, her husband's), and even more difficult to be approving of it.

Three years since our first important decision as a family, the dust has settled a little. My husband's parents send postcards from their vacations addressed to Emily Buchanan, telling her about all the places they are visiting that they would love her to see with them when she is older. We get the occasional package from my parents addressed to Emily Binenbaum Buchanan, which I suppose represents some progress. And I think, after a few years of living with it, that both sides are ultimately proud of our choice. My daughter's having my last name raises eyebrows in some places—what, are you not married, did you get divorced, does your husband not love you—but when I tell other moms, especially the ones who kept their own names, the reaction is more of amazement: wow, you can actually *do* that? Our relatives and others at first seemed to think that it's the name that makes you a family, that having separate names makes it easier to divorce, to leave, to fall apart. But it's not a single name that unifies us, that keeps us together through some invisible force. It's living and working and compromising together, day after day, honoring one another and fuming at one another, and despite everything loving one another, no matter what our names sound like when you say them aloud.

Mother Tongue

I didn't always use foul language. In fact, until I was in college, I don't think I used anything stronger than the word "hell" in mixed company. When I was a seventeen-year-old piano student, a freshman at the Boston Conservatory, my prudishness was an endless source of amusement for my friends. Chris, a cellist from New Zealand, used to torture me over my "innocence," forbidding me to enter the practice floor until I uttered a profanity.

"Come on," he'd goad me. "I'll start you out easy. Just say, 'It's freezing here.'"

"It's freezing here," I'd oblige.

"Okay, now say, 'It's FUCKING freezing here!'"

At which point I would blush and hilarity would ensue. Eventually I'd admit that it was, indeed, fucking freezing on the practice floor, and he'd say, "See, that wasn't so bad, was it?"

Oh, if Chris could hear me now.

I'm not sure when it was that I morphed from a grammatically correct prude into a trash-talking freak, but my old Conservatory friends would now be proud to hear the way I swear over everything from being woken up in the middle of the night to realizing I've left the wet clothes in the washer for three days. At this point, "fuck" isn't even a swear word anymore; sentences just don't sound right unless it's interspersed somewhere.

I'm not proud of this. As someone who edits and writes for a meager living, I know I should have more respect for the spoken word, and I do manage to restrain myself from tossing around profanities at my daughter's playschool or when talking on the phone in a professional capacity. But I admit that at home, when no visitors are present, all bets are off. Even when I try to rein it in in front of my daughter, things occasionally slip out.

The first time I heard Emi utter a profanity was when she was almost two and a half, and it was a doozy. I was working at the computer on a tight deadline and she was playing "kitchen" next to me. Suddenly my computer froze up just as I tried to CTRL-S all the edits I'd just input. To my credit, all I yelled was "Oh, MAN!!!"

"What happened, Mommy?" Emi asked, concerned.

"Oh, sweetie, nothing really—my computer just broke a little and now I have to fix it."

"Oh," she said, and shrugged her shoulders. "Fuck it!"

I know I shouldn't have, but I burst out laughing. Once I got myself together we had a brief conversation about words grown-ups say when they're frustrated, and we came up with a nice list of silly things we could say instead of "fuck": shimmy-shammy, silly, blither-blather. . . . And we talked about words we could say inside the house and words that people outside don't really like to hear. She agreed that it was probably a good idea to use silly words instead of the grown-up ones.

"I not say 'fuck it' in a eva-lator," she told me. "I say 'shimmy-shammy.'"

"Okay, that sounds like a great idea," I said.

Then she looked at me with a solemn expression and told me, "Daddy say, 'Fuck it.'"

Secretly vindicated that I wasn't the only culprit, I told her we'd all try to remember to say shimmy-shammy instead of that other word, even Daddy.

"Yeah," she said. "People in a eva-lator don't like-a hear us say 'Fuck it.' Old ladies don't like it."

No, old ladies certainly don't like it, I agreed.

"Old ladies don't like-a hear me say 'ass' too. I say 'BUTT!'"

"Oh, uh, wow," I stammered, "That's probably a good idea."

"Yeah. And I not say 'boobies' either. Old ladies don't like it," she told me. "Not in a eva-lator."

No, indeed.

Growing up in my parents' house, swearing was not an option. There were bad words and there were good words, and bad words were words that good people didn't use. The one time I can remember using a swear word as a kid was when I was five or six and a friend kept knocking on the door and asking if I could come out and play despite the fact that my mom had told us both that I could not. After the fourth or fifth time the friend knocked, I slammed the door in frustration and yelled, "Damn that Jenny!"

My mom, shocked, said, "Don't *ever* say that! Who told you to say that?! Where did you hear that?"

And I, following the traditional after-school-special/ anti-drug-commercial script, burst into tears, crying, "I heard it from you!"

In sharp contrast to this was the household my husband was raised in. Profanities flowed freely, and it was a regular dinnertime game to see who could get his mom to sigh the loudest over the language she'd overhear.

Sitting quietly, my husband's sister would get his attention.

"Hey, Gil," she'd say.

"What?"

"Pass the fucking corn."

To which he'd reply, "Hey, Rona."

"Yeah?"

"Here's the fucking corn."

Then their dad would say, "Kids, stop talking about the fucking corn!" At which point their mother would burst into tears, put her head in her hands, and sigh as loudly as possible, saying, "I can't take this anymore! Why do you talk to each other this way?!" And the three of them—my husband, his sister, and their dad—would start laughing so hard, they were crying. Ten years ago I would have been horrified to have been a witness to those dinner conversations. Now, I'm afraid, I would fit right in.

After Emi's first exploration into the vocabulary of the profane, I resolved to try to curb my foul mouth. She seemed to get the concept of inside versus outside words, or words that were okay to say at home but not so appropriate to say in front of old ladies in the "eva-lator," but still it seemed a good idea to cut down on the confusion and stop swearing altogether.

I thought I had done a decent job of watching my mouth, and of not giving Emi much of a reaction when she'd try out a "mommy-daddy word" on me, but when she was almost three, I realized the damage was probably already done.

We were all in the car, coming home from the grocery store, and I was in the back with Emi, trying to help her dress her panda in a bracelet and necklace. "I do it!" she demanded, so I backed off and watched her struggle. Finally, after several unsuccessful attempts to get the necklace on Panda, she yelled, "Fuck, Mommy! I can't fucking do it!!!!"

Gil almost swerved off the road. "Did she just say what I think she said?"

"YEAH," Emi yelled, "I CAN'T FUCKING DO IT!!!"

I think we were both filled with an equal mixture of pride

and shame—there she was, our beautiful daughter, swearing with a profane maturity I myself did not reach until I was well into my twenties . . . and yet, there she was, our beautiful daughter, uttering words no nearly three-year-old should know how to say, let alone use in a sentence. We were both awed and ashamed.

I eventually stopped laughing and calmed down enough to say, "Wow, I bet you heard Mommy or Daddy say something like that when we were really frustrated. Can you think of some other words that Emi and Mommy and Daddy can say instead? Because I bet it would be more fun to say something really silly."

"Yeah!" she giggled, and started up with her list of silly nonsense words as she went back to the task of getting Panda's necklace on. I, meanwhile, was silently congratulating myself on my smoothness in handling the incident, patting myself on the back for not making her feel ashamed for saying something she had no idea was not appropriate to say, and for steering her into a more socially acceptable alternative without the stigma of my disapproval. Somehow, despite our vastly different upbringings, my husband and I had turned out okay. Perhaps, I thought, taking the middle way with our daughter would be an acceptable alternative to washing our mouths out with soap and starting over.

My reverie of parental mastery was suddenly interrupted by my daughter, who was still attempting to get the necklace on Panda.

"Fuck, Mommy!" she yelled. "I STILL can't fucking do this!!!!"

Oh, shimmy-shammy.

Don't get the wrong idea: we are not proud to be walking this fine line of linguistic inappropriateness. But a surprisingly good thing that has sprung from the fact of our bad-word usage is that at a tender age, Emi understands the concept of context. She has become preternaturally attuned to the social aspect of language, the subtleties of what is appropriate when we use words to express ourselves in social interaction. Hearing Gil swear under his breath as he realizes he's stepped in gum on the hot city sidewalk, she'll command, "Don't say that word outside! People don't like to hear it!" Overhearing a playmate's mom in conversation saying, "I'd better get my ass in gear," Emi corrects her, "Don't say 'ass'! People don't like it! Say 'BUTT' instead!" She understands the concept of public and private vocabulary.

Of course, now that she is a budding preschooler, she is learning words that are even more loaded than "mommy-daddy words:" she's learning those little-kid "bad words" like "stupid" and "poopy-head" and other delightfully nasty-sounding potty talk. We have conversations about those words too, about words you can say for a joke at home and words that might hurt someone's feelings if you said them at school. I'm fine with that, for now—relieved, even, to hear the normal, age-appropriate verbal insults coming from her rather than the kind adults yell at each other in traffic. I suppose it's only a matter of time before she combines all her powerful adult and child bad-word vocabulary into one hellaciously offensive epithet. Hopefully, by then she'll also be away at college, amusing her classmates with her trash-talking ease, and gently teasing someone who started out like me, unable to swear without blushing.

Everything I Really Needed to Know
I Learned at Playgroup

I t's 8:15 A.M., on any day of my daughter's first year-and a half of life, when my phone rings. I know even before I answer it that it's Shawna, calling to make a plan for the day.

"Hey, it's Shawna," she says when I answer the phone. I can hear Zack screaming in the background. "We've been up since five this morning, how about you?"

"Six," I tell her over Emi's whining.

She groans. "You're so lucky!" I hear her muffled voice telling Zack to calm down, that she'll be off the phone soon. Then she is back. "I think we've already seen this damn *Barney* tape eight times this morning!"

"Right there with you," I say with an eye on the *Blue's Clues* episode Emi has watched continuously since waking two hours ago.

"So, what are you up for? The Please Touch? The Dinosaur Museum? Should we hit the park before it gets too hot?" Every weekday morning we weigh our options like this, and each morning we realize anew the pros and cons of each one. The children's museum, which is properly known as the Please Touch Museum and imprudently known as the Please Give Me an Ear Infection Museum, is wonderful—but only as long as you and your baby or toddler arrive the second the doors open, before the influx of rowdy school groups. Being there first thing not only gives you free rein of the place; an early-morning arrival has the added bonus of making it entirely possible that your kid may be the first one of the day to suck on whatever he or she grabs off the many touchable, temptingly chewable exhibits. The Dinosaur Museum is actually the Academy of Natural Sciences, and it, too, is a decent kiddie activity (despite the fact that the dinosaurs there are "just a bunch of bones," as one perceptive child pointed out when we were there recently). The caveat with that place is again a timely arrival to avoid the older schoolchildren on field trips. But also important to keep in mind is that there's only so much to do there when your child is under the age of two, so if it's a whole morning you're looking to while away, you may have to come up with other options. And as for the park, well, figuring out whether to go involves a delicate equation that takes into consideration variables such as the day's weather, which park and what distance it is from the house, toddler temperament, and overall maternal energy level.

"Oh, gosh, I don't know," I sigh. "I don't think I can face the park today." Memories from our last venture there—tears over having to share toys, falls from poorly designed climbing structures, shoves from oblivious grade-schoolers, refusal to eat any snack resulting in hunger-induced melt-down, returning home with dirt in every possible crevice yet stubbornly renouncing bathtime—are still too fresh to revisit. "How about the dinosaurs?"

"Zack gets kinda bored there," she tells me.

"Okay, well, if we leave in the next fifteen minutes we can make it to the Please Touch by 9:00. Are you up for that?"

"Why not?" she says. "Okay, I'll call Karen and Monica, you call Maria and Paula. Is Elise around today? Oh, that's right, she's working. All right, so I'll see you on the corner of 22nd and Locust at like 8:45? And maybe after the museum, after nap time, we can grab lunch, do the library baby story hour, and then hang in the Square?" Shawna is the organizer of the group, whipping us all into action.

"Sounds good," I say, and hang up the phone. Relief sweeps over me: we have a plan for the day, and I won't have to be alone.

It's a wonderful thing to know five to ten other moms who live within blocks of me, whose numbers I know by heart, whom I can call in the too-early hours of the morning to save me from the blankness of the day that looms ahead. Especially in that bleary first year of mothering, having other moms to plan with saved me from the inertia of a house-bound routine. I had an artsy-craftsy mom friend I could count on to come up with fun projects to do with empty baby-food jars on rainy days; I had a spur-of-the-moment mom friend I knew would have something exciting and unanticipated going on whenever I chanced to call; I had a serious mom friend I could talk to about serious non-mom things—I had a mom friend for nearly every occasion, and it was comforting to know that my daughter and I were just a phone call away from impromptu playdates and afternoon activities.

"It's the stroller brigade," people would say to us as we barreled down the street, three or four or five of us briskly walking the city in a pack. And we were, a brigade of women with babies, with strollers packed for every possible situation, be it inclement weather, excessive pooping, play-time accidents, or the need for toys or snacks; a stroller brigade determined to transport ourselves through the long, lonely days of mommy life.

As a math-challenged writer type, I always disagreed with the old saw "there is safety in numbers." Numbers didn't make me feel safe, numbers didn't make sense to me; words did. And even taking the phrase the way it was meant to be interpreted didn't work, as I was always more comfortable by myself than in well-populated social situations. But as a mom, I suddenly saw the value of it: the more of us there were, the less the individual burden of caring for our children. The more I was surrounded by other moms, the greater the chance that if I had forgotten the wipes again or failed to pack lunch, someone else would have remembered. The greater the chance that if I was exhausted and sleep-deprived, someone else would have energy to spare. On the days I couldn't get a chuckle out of Emi, Karen would have her laughing until she had the hiccups. On the days I couldn't get Emi to eat anything, Shawna would manage to get her to try something she'd never eat at home. With other moms around, I had help, I had relief— I had backup. And so did they.

Hanging out with other moms was also a nice reality check. It was reassuring to see that other kids went through the same stages mine did, it was instructive to see how each mother dealt with the developmental and behavioral things that came up. And even the practical matters proved to be enlightening: I caught on to the concept of snacks only after watching all the other moms break out their little Ziplocs and Tupperware containers full of cereal or pretzels or nutritious things for their kids to munch on. I learned everything from where the good dollar stores were to what the best baby music class was to what effective techniques for handling toddler tantrums might be. And our babies had instant friends right from the beginning. Three years after our first official meeting, though some of our original group has moved away, Emi still plays with friends she has known since she was just a few months old.

Before Emi was born, I didn't know any moms nearby. I didn't even know anyone else who was pregnant. Partially this was because I was new in town, and partially it was because I worked from home, so the only pregnant woman I had occasion to see on a daily basis was the one staring back at me when I looked in the mirror, marveling at the ability of my stomach to stretch beyond what I'd thought was humanly possible. But this being the virtual age, I found a community of other new mothers-to-be online. Right there in my house, at my desk, at my fingertips, there was an invisible collection of other women fumbling toward motherhood just like me.

I posted on the mom-to-be discussion boards frequently and came to know a number of women due around my delivery date. I began to find myself talking about them in normal, nonvirtual conversation—saying random things like, "One of my friends had an ultrasound yesterday and found out she's carrying twins!" or "I know someone due the same day as me who's on bedrest." My mother-in-law commented finally, "That's amazing that you have so many friends who are pregnant! How do you know all these people?" And my husband jumped right in. "They're from this Web site. My guess is they're all really forty-five-year-old guys sitting around in their underwear."

They weren't, though the site did have its fair share of what in message-board lingo are referred to as trolls—people posting, sometimes under false pretenses, solely to stir things up, create controversy, and attract attention. In fact, over the course of my pregnancy, delivery, and early experience of motherhood with Emi, the original group of women I began posting with spun off through four different message boards, until the problem of trolling and personality conflict was solved altogether by forming an e-mail discussion group rather than a public board.

Once my daughter was born, the virtual playgroup became a companion to the actual playgroup that I became a part of. In the actual playgroup, I had real-life, face-to-face interactions with other moms and babies. I had people to call for help if I needed it, friends to hang out with when I desperately needed a break from the baby babble. I learned the practical aspects of motherhood from them, the geographically specific facts of daily mom-life in our city. The virtual playgroup afforded me a wider range of mothering experiences as I traded posts and e-mails with women from around the country and around the world, in all different economic, social, and psychological states. In the virtual group, though we all got to know one another well after months and then years of posting about pregnancy, delivery, and life with a newborn, we were protected by anonymity. Few of us had actually seen any of the others in person, and there was a measure of comfort there. It's far easier to type away to a group of strangers about a husband's affair, scarily persistent anxiety attacks, or a child's developmental delay than it is to show up and talk about those things with people who see you nearly every day. So the virtual playgroup was the psyche of my early motherhood, the real-life playgroup the physical embodiment of it. I needed them both.

Both groups—the real-life one and the virtual one—had the kind of sub-groups, cliques, and personality conflicts you might expect when large numbers of people get together. In the real-life group, there were sub-groups of moms who lived near each other and who hung out together more often than those who lived in different neighborhoods. There were people who clicked with one another and people who didn't, just like in other kinds of social gatherings. Online, the group was larger and more varied, so there were more subdivisions, and instead of being grouped by neighborhoods or geography, women became grouped by their politics or parenting choices: breast-feeders versus bottle feeders, attachment-parenting moms versus more traditional moms. The major difference between my real-life group and the online experience was that the non-virtual playgroup was limited geographically and temporally: we were moms living in Philly, and while we might call each other early in the mornings to make plans, if we were up in the dead of night, or desperate in the wee hours of the morning, we were on our own. My virtual playgroup was always open. I could post a message at 3:00 A.M. and more often than not someone else would be around—awake like me or in a whole other time zone in another country on an entirely new day—to commiserate or post back later. And if I was tired of my usual board, there were a million others in cyber, space to choose from: alternative-parenting boards, punk-rock-mama boards, political-activist-mom boards, boards for moms who want to talk about how they plan to decorate their kids' rooms, boards for moms addicted to buying and selling things on eBay, niche parenting boards for moms of every ideology. The invisible network of my online group of mothers was as comforting as the knowledge that I had a network of real friends to depend on, and between the two I felt covered, emotionally protected, safe within the sheer number of other moms I knew who were experiencing what I was experiencing.

Now that our kids are in playschool or preschool until lunchtime, I rarely get those early-morning calls from my mom friends in town, desperate to make pre-lunchtime plans. Instead, it's all about filling the afternoons. We call one another from our cell phones and make plans to meet for lunch at the park, to play at one another's houses, to do an afternoon trip to the same old museums, to visit air-conditioned bookstores. Some of Emi's friends still nap, so Emi and I hang out by ourselves for those midday hours, or we get together with other moms and preschoolers who somehow manage to stay awake the whole day.

In the beginning, when our babies were babies, meeting up with the other moms for activities was more about us moms than it was about the kids. It was an excuse to talk and share our experiences, to get out of our houses and feel adult and human again, our babies snoozing or feeding or otherwise doing baby things while we socialized. After a certain point, once our kids were a little bigger, our meetings became more about the children playing together and learning how to be social. Now that our kids are older, verbal, and past the worst of the possessive not-sharing stage, it's almost back to the way it was at the beginning. We can sit and talk over a cup of coffee, trading stories from our lives, while the kids amuse one another, inventing games, doing silly dancing, or play-acting their favorite stories. And my virtual conversations with my online mom friends are like that too. We still compare notes, trade cute kid stories, talk about potty training and night terrors and whether it's time for baby number two (or, in some cases, three), but now we also talk about the extra-maternal things we are doing now that we have some time to do them. We talk about our jobs, our lives, our spouses, goals that we have that have absolutely nothing to do with our children.

Both of my playgroups started out as support networks for surviving early motherhood, but over the years they have evolved into something even stronger: a family of sorts, the now-clichéd "village" that it is supposed to take to raise a child. They are my lifelines of support, proof that other people understand what it's like to be where I am, learning how to be a mother. The moms I have met both virtually and in real life have been there for my daughter's first steps, for my first flush of confidence as a new mom, for the occasions in our lives that have been both joyous and disappointing. Often, when something exciting happens, these friends are the first people I tell. And on those days when I feel overwhelmed by the circumstances of my life, I know they are there, just a late-night e-mail or an early-morning phone call away.

Learning to Speak

When I was about nine and my younger sister was eight, our youngest sister was four. She was the baby of the family, and she was treasured accordingly, though of course being the littlest she did get her share of torture from us. I remember all of us riding in the car with my mom at the wheel, on our way to gymnastics or chorus practice or piano lessons or some other extracurricular activity. We all sat in the back, sitting close together so as better to play our favorite game, "Corners," which basically consisted of leaning on each other as the station wagon rounded a curve, smooshing the person closest to the door, and yelling at the top of our lungs, "Corners!" As my mom took a sharp right and the car veered, we all toppled together, and my little sister yelled out, "Corners!"—or, as she pronounced it at the time, "Kworners!"

My other sister and I laughed in derision. "'Kworners' ? What's 'kworners'?"

"That's how I say it," our little sister told us.

"What, do you eat KWORN for dinner?" one of us said.

"Yeah, do you drink KWOOL-AID?" taunted the other.

"That's enough!" yelled my mom from the front seat.

"COR-ners," my little sister said tentatively. "See, I DO say it right! COR-ners."

My mom fairly slammed on the brakes. "Oh, thanks, you two," she snapped. "You just teased her right out of one of my favorite things she says. You just took away the last vestige of her babyhood. Thanks a lot!"

"Sheesh, what's the big deal?" I muttered under my breath as I watched my little sister silently trying out her new pronunciation.

Now that I'm a mom, I understand.

When you have a new baby, you spend the first few months of its life basically talking to yourself, often in a high-pitched voice and often in the form of questions. It's kind of like being on *Jeopardy!*, with the additional rules that you are required to speak in a singsong voice and that your only choice of category is "Things You Might be Embarrassed to Say in the Presence of Another Adult." You say things like: "Who's a good girl?" "Did you see the wittle bunny?" "Who's my good eater?" "Where's Mommy's nose?" "Did you make that good burpie?" or "Who's my big pooper?" I remember the first time I realized my daughter actually understood some of what I was incessantly babbling about.

She was about eight months old, and we were doing our usual daytime thing: hanging out, me talking in that singsong voice, asking questions to fill the silence, with her response being a big-eyed, drooling, blank stare. Suddenly I realized it was lunchtime, so I said, "Emi! Do you know what time it is?" Her eyes lit up in anticipation. "Lunchtime!" I answered for her, and placed her in her high chair. To my surprise, she burst into tears, a worried, confused expression on her face. "What?" I asked her. "What's wrong? It's lunchtime, sweetie, it's time to eat lunch!" And then it hit me: I had gotten into the habit of prefacing her daily bath— bathtime being Emi's favorite activity at that point—by always asking, "Do you know what time it is?" and then responding excitedly, "BATHTIME!"

Had she really expected me to say "bathtime" instead of "lunchtime"? Was that why she was upset?

"Oh, sweetie, did you think I was going to say bathtime, is that why you're crying?" I asked her, though I knew an actual response would not be forthcoming.

"Ba!" she said through her tears. "Baaaaaa!"

I was stunned. She had been paying attention to my babbling all along. The correct answer to "do you know what time it is?" was indeed "bathtime," not "lunchtime." She was right.

"Ba!" she said again, louder.

It was her first real word, and I postponed lunch in favor of an afternoon bath that day to show her I understood.

"Ba" became the gateway word to other words. At first, many of them sounded similar: a bus might also provoke her to say "ba," as might a balloon or the sight of her bottle. But there were barely detectable differences in inflection that no one other than she or I could understand, and that made all the difference. "Bus" had more of an "uh" sound to it, "balloon" had more of a staccato delivery, "bottle" was often indicated by the excited repetition of "ba-ba-ba!" as opposed to the drawn-out "aaa" sound of "ba" when she meant "bath." Soon she moved on to other vowel sounds. "Bee" meant "push" as well as the actual insect. "Bye" meant goodbye, just the way you might assume it would. Eventually, she had a whole vocabulary of Emi-speak, sounds that communicated what she was trying to explain without necessarily resembling actual words in the English language.

As she grew older, some of her vocabulary became more understandable, but we still had to hand out crib-sheet translations for the grandparents and playschool teachers. "Aysees" was "A-B-Cs," "bla-blee" was "broccoli," "Clues clues" was "Blue's Clues," "doo-day, you-you" was "happy birthday to you," "help-oo" was "help you," which actually meant "help me." For a year or more, she referred to herself as "Mimi," and for nearly that long she used the expression "mo want" to communicate that she wanted more of something. (The construction took on a life of its own, though, and soon "mo want" became the necessary thing to say not only for wanting more but for when she wanted anything at all. "Mo want dat!" she'd command. "Mo want dis!" "Who's Mo?" we'd ask her. "And why does he want all this stuff?")

Once her speech really picked up, she developed an excited stutter as she tried to get the words out as fast as she was thinking them. After a while, everyone pretty much got the hang of deciphering her baby talk, and all of us, Mommy and Daddy and Grandma and Grandpa alike—that's "Manga and Bapa" to the two-year-old Emi, but "Grandma and Grandpa" to her at age two and a half—often found ourselves falling into using her vocabulary ourselves.

But the Emi-speak is fleeting, as I learned a while back when I offered Emi some of her favorite fruit, asking her if she was hungry for some "pope-pope." "Mommy, it's not pope-pope!" she laughed. "It's *cantaloupe!*" And as I realized again just this month when she told me, "Mommy, I say 'caterpillar' now that I'm a big girl; I not say 'calla-pillar' anymore." She is as proud of her grown-up pronunciation (though she still says "growm-up") as I am nostalgic for her baby words, and I try to praise her even as I mourn the passing of such gems as "a-body" for "somebody" and "all-body" for "everybody," "kir-koys" for "circles," and "lemma-lade" for "lemonade."

At age three, she is shedding her baby words as quickly as her baby fat. She is less likely to devolve into Emi-speak and more likely to express herself in surprising sentences like "Mommy, you look interesting today" or "Mommy, you think about it and then you buy me those shoes" or "I was dreaming about it snowing and I gave all my friends yellow chairs in the snow" or "Mommy, your boobies look like raindrops." She still says "bed-night" for "bed-time" and elevators are still "eva-lators"; she still accomplishes amazing feats "all my-byself" and requests to stay up and read books or watch videos for "just a little bittit," but I know these vestiges of her early life are marked for extinction.

Luckily, now that I am no longer just a torturing older sister but a mom, there is no chance that I will tease her out of them.

IV

Mother Land

Adjustment. The sojourner begins to work in and enjoy the new culture, though there may be occasional instances of anxiety and strain.

—Kalvero Oberg

Adaptation or Biculturalism: Full recovery will result in an ability to function in two cultures with confidence. You will even find a great many customs, ways of doing and saying things, and personal attitudes that you enjoy—indeed, to which you have in some degree acculturated—and that you will definitely miss when you pack up and return home.

—The University of Iowa's Web site on culture shock

I have learned to get along on very little sleep. Most of all I have learned to love. To say that having a baby changes your life is a great, great understatement. Having a baby explodes your life and you may not be able to find your old self among the pieces. I remember the girl I was before I was a mother. I thought that if only I had this or if only I had that I would be happy. I look back at that silly young girl with compassion—I think of her almost the way I would think of a daughter. —Susan Cheever

Often as a parent raising children, . . . I have wished for a guidebook, a map to direct me through the labyrinth of the human emotional field, to cleanly and gracefully assist my children through the hills and valleys of achievements and failures. I have learned that the only guidebook of any effectiveness is the human heart. —Joy Harjo

Motherhood is like Albania—you can't trust the descriptions in the books, you have to go there. —Marni Jackson

Not Like Mozart

Nothing, really, is like mothering except mothering. You can baby-sit or be a nanny, and that can be your ticket into the nonstop show that is caring for a child, but the fact is that you get paid to be there, and at the end of the day you get to go home by yourself and sleep. You can be responsible for a younger sibling as you grow up, but even then you are exempt from the psychological complexities of a true parent-child relationship. These experiences and others can prepare you for mothering, to some extent. But you won't really find out what it's like until you're already there.

In my pre-mom life, I was a pianist. When I entered into the crucible of my professional training, the conservatory I attended in Boston, it was my first real experience in the world of serious music. I had always been someone who did a lot of things at once, and it was strange to suddenly have to be focused on one thing and one thing only. Even scarier, I was to be evaluated solely on how I did that one thing. No one there much cared if I could write or sing or tap dance or carry five full dinner plates at the same time: all they wanted to hear from me was piano playing, and damn good playing at that.

I practiced in isolation, hours at a time, working invisibly, doing repetitive things for hours on end. Scales. Arpeggios. That octave passage in the Chopin. The trill in the Mozart sonata that was kicking my ass. Things that I knew I would have to return to the next day, and the next, practicing over and over and over until problem spots were no longer problem spots and my brain could breeze right through them and all my fingers had to do was play. I struggled to understand what my teacher kept trying to tell me about having a beginner's mind: practicing and practicing, all so I could play whatever I was playing with the same fresh perspective I'd had the very first time I played it.

I was remembering this the other day the way you might remember a dream you had a few weeks ago or a movie you saw when you were in college. It was hard to reconcile that memory of myself and my life with the person I am now. Sitting with my daughter at the piano while she showed me the low notes and the high notes, I wondered for a moment whether my life as a mom does somehow relate to my life then, whether my hard, invisible work from those years had some purpose other than whatever concert I was preparing for at the time.

When I think about it, the daily work of mothering is

similar to the work of music. The work I do as a mother is repetitive and mostly invisible, just like practicing piano. I make food and then it is eaten. I clean dishes and then they are crusted with leftovers. I do the laundry and the clothes are dirty again. I dust and the house is dusty. I clean up toys that are thrown down as soon as I pick them up; I change diapers and give baths, wipe noses, and wash hands. My days are endless rituals of things continually done and undone, just as my experience of practicing piano was one of constant raveling and unraveling, constructing and deconstructing.

But mothering is not music. For one thing, music was never so demanding, never so frustrating, never so all-consuming. Sure, it had its moments, but Beethoven never woke me up five times a night, Mozart never pooped on me, I never had to clean up Prokofiev's puke. As a musician I was laboring to resolve my own issues, not taking care of someone else's. It was always a choice to practice or not practice; it is never a choice to not feed or not clothe or not love. So while I felt compelled, in a sense, to do the work of music, the work of mothering is a different kind of compulsion altogether.

The terror of failing, though, is almost the same. The shock I had upon entering the conservatory and discovering that no one cared about my various abilities (aside from the one I had been admitted to refine) was revisited when my daughter was born. She couldn't know, as a tiny newborn, that my intentions were good. She couldn't care that I was trying to do a million things at once. All that mattered to her was what I actually did: that I came when she cried, that I met her needs, that I took care of her. I had to do just one thing, mother her, and I had to do it perfectly. This, too, is an important difference between music and mothering: for all its importance in the moment of performance, a Mozart sonata is not a living thing, and it is not of much consequence if I flub a note or two. But my daughter is a different creation entirely, and my lack of practice has a much more serious impact.

Back when I first started at the conservatory, I had a cassette tape I would listen to when my roommates were away: Glenn Gould playing Brahms. It sounded powerful, haunted, rich, and thick. I'd turn up the volume so that the music would vibrate the thin walls as it played, as if I could render its meaning through sheer loudness. I did not know then how to listen. Every chord, every mysterious, surprising harmonic progression, made sense to me not musically, not logically, but emotionally. I was reacting to the music but not understanding it, nodding my head as if it made sense but not really knowing why. I would lie on my bed, submerged in sound, and imagine the music seeping into me and making meaning of its own accord.

Later, when I was twenty and moving across coasts to graduate school, I came across the tape and listened to it once again. What a different experience. I was listening with trained ears, hearing tone and balance and phrasing, thinking music theory, envisioning the physicality of playing it. All the mysteries made sense, and in their place was a curious nostalgia for whatever it was that had made the piece sound so mysterious to me before.

I'd like to think that my experience of becoming a musician prepared me for the work I'm doing now. I'd like to think the stamina, the patience, the focus I honed then, has weathered the transition from Mozart-player to mama and is with me here on the other side. I'd like to think I still have access to that beginner's mind, which in mom-life means the ability to see each diaper change, each chore, each meal, each bath, each demand as a new thing, a separate thing, a unique thing, a thing not done and yet not undone. So I try to hold on to the memory of those early days when my daughter and I were still strangers to each other. I try to remember the newness of it all, the uncertainty, the unfamiliarity—and most of all the awe, like the mystery of that music I would slowly come to understand, filling me up with emotion, vibrating the walls, and seeping into every pore.

Fall Back

I am a big fan of sleep. Sleep is amazing, sleep is wonderful, sleep, as the kids would say, rocks. So I have always been a big fan of "Fall Back." I mean, what's not to like about turning back the clocks and getting an extra hour of sleep? The only downside of Fall Back was always the dreaded Spring Forward, which seemed not only unnecessary but downright cruel. Lose an hour of sleep? Who came up with that idea, and why did everyone go along with it?

Now that I am a mom, however, it is Fall Back that is the cruel joke: non-parents around the country (in those compliant states, anyway) get to savor the joy of sleeping an extra hour, snoozing unaccosted through sixty precious bonus minutes of soporific heaven. But not me, not anymore. You see, babies haven't been briefed on the whole daylight-saving-time thing, and neither have toddlers. In fact, I don't think the whole new-human-being concept was focus-grouped enough in the first place: babies and toddlers don't grasp the idea of eight to twelve straight hours of uninterrupted sleep; they don't come with teeth; they're incontinent; in the beginning they can't even control their limbs. Who would sign up for that given the option of having instead a little tiny person who springs from the womb fully equipped to sleep all night and maybe even whip up her own breakfast in the morning?

Which brings me back to the whole Fall Back thing. Where I used to look forward to it, I now dread it, knowing that not only will I be summoned in the night for more drink, more *Bear in the Big Blue House* CD, more stuffed animal who fell out of bed, more please touch my head till I fall asleep again, but I'll also be summoned with a raging cry of "MOM-MAY!!!! COME HERE NOW!!!"—and just in case I was thinking of sending in an emissary in my place, "NO DADDY!!!"—a full hour earlier than normal, which is already plenty early enough.

Pre-baby I used to fantasize about winning the lottery, or becoming deliriously famous and rich. Now I fantasize about sleep. I fantasize about slumber the way guys fantasize about sex. Hours of it, days of it. Sleeping on the couch, on the bed, on the floor, wherever I can find a comfortable spot. It is almost illicit, so decadent and unimaginable, it now seems to sleep when I want, where I want, and for as long as I want.

Here's a little sordid tidbit about my former life: when I was eighteen, I became really sick. No one was sure what it was, so I just called it Mystery Disease, and I went from doctor to doctor in an effort to figure out what the heck was wrong with me. The basic problem was this constant pain that felt like shin splints all over my body, and it was so wearying that pretty much all I could do was sleep. When it first started, I remember I went to sleep one Friday afternoon and woke up on Sunday, nearly forty-eight hours later. I regularly slept eighteen hours, twenty-four hours at a stretch. I would always still be in pain when I woke up, and I would always still be incredibly tired.

At the time, it was devastating: I had to complete a year of college from my bed in the dorm, I was achy and tired like a middle-aged lady, and I feared that instead of going out with friends and having a normal social life I'd be doomed to going to the local diners at 4:30 so as not to miss the early bird special like the rest of the folks with my energy level. It took five years of this, this pain and this bone-tired fatigue, before I received the catch-all diagnosis of chronic fatigue syndrome, and by that time I was getting better. By the time I finished graduate school, I had only intermittent pain, I had energy, and I wasn't tired anymore. It eventually went away as mysteriously as it began, and after a year or so of being consciously thankful for having energy and being pain free, I went back to my normal state of not appreciating the difference.

Once I finally recovered, I thought of that sleep-filled period of my life as something to be kept secret—something a little embarrassing, something indicative of my personal flaws in general. But now that I have been in varying stages of sleep-deprivation for about two and a half years (not coincidentally the length of time that I have also been a mother)—now I look back on that time as my glory days. And in a way perhaps I needed it. Maybe those five years of marathon sleeping stocked me up for the intermittent sleep patterns of these early years of motherhood. Maybe without those nearly decade-old reserves I'd be even crankier when awoken for the fourth time in a single night (though according to my husband, that's not possible).

Fall Back reminds me of the days when I slept with abandon the way Valentine's Day might fondly remind someone else of an old lover: in retrospect the tough times seem less difficult, the good times even rosier, the follies of youth tender and sweet instead of merely embarrassing now that we are old enough to be kind in our judgment. My shameful sleeping days of the past now resemble my current sleeping fantasies, and I'm finally just beginning to know for sure the way these things go: one of these days I'll have my Fall Back sleep all to myself again, no little voice to stir me from my slumber, no tiny body to clamor for a hug, no "I love you, Mommy" visits in the middle of the night—and I'll miss them.

Forgetting

Our capacity to forget is amazing.

I still remember being in labor, thinking to myself, "This is the hardest thing I've ever done. If I can get through this pain, I can get through anything!" Yet the next day I whimpered like a newborn when the nurses came in to rip off the bandages securing my IV. I still remember those sleepless nights of early motherhood, when I'd get no more than twenty minutes of rest in between successive bouts of feeding/crying/diapering, telling myself, "I will NEVER do this again!" And yet now I occasionally see a cute, gurgling, chubby, happy baby and think to myself, "Hmm . . . it wasn't really that bad, was it?"

I suppose it's a useful defense mechanism to forget your pain and difficulties; otherwise how would we keep on going? Who would birth more children, stay up with them through sleepless nights? Of course, we tend to forget the good stuff too: it's hard to remember that the kid who's flailing and screaming in a monumental temper tantrum is the same one who gave you a big juicy hug yesterday and said, "I love you, Mommy!" for the first time. Whether it's pain or joy, once it's gone, we lose the heat of the moment. We become lulled by the routine of daily life. We forget.

I wrestle with this forgetting, because there are things I want to remember. So I try to write things down, I try to think about them as they happen. And because I've scribbled a few words or reminded myself of something, I foolishly think I have staved off forgetting—until, suddenly, life reminds me that I have not.

My daughter took her nap later than usual today—for one thing, she slept late (oh, it's not as great as it sounds: she was up about four times in the night just wanting company); and for another, she was being so darn cute I just couldn't bear to start the nap war. All she wanted to do was to sit on the couch with me and "do books." She didn't want me to read to her, she wanted me to sit with my book and read silently while she sat next to me with her book, "reading" silently.

She picked out books for both of us and commanded me to sit down on a specific part of the couch. She gave me "my" book, Spalding Gray's *Morning, Noon and Night*, and said, "Mommy read dere!" Then she sat down with "her" book, *TV Guide*, and said, "Emi read here!" We read that way for about fifteen minutes. Every once in a while I'd turn my head to look at her, but she'd push my cheek so that my face was forward again and say, "Listen! Read words!" Often, when she'd do this, I'd laugh, and I was happy that instead of being sensitive about it, she laughed along with me. The one time I didn't laugh, she commanded, "Mommy, LAUGH!" So that was good. Usually she says, "No funny! No joke! No laughing!"

Finally I realized if I didn't try to get her to sleep, it would be a horrible afternoon. Ninety-five degrees in the shade plus humidity plus cranky toddler equals one very long day indoors. So I put her in the stroller, gave her her bunny and her panda, grabbed my keys and the cell, and headed out. My usual track is to just walk up a few blocks, then turn around and come home. Usually that's all it takes, though sometimes I've had to walk miles. So I started on my usual schlep, took care of a few calls while maneuvering the stroller, and she fell asleep by the time I hit the park. I turned around and started home.

When we got to the corner where her playschool is, I stopped for the light and was startled to see, about three hundred feet in front of me, a huge white truck—smaller than a semi, bigger than a tow truck, but with one of those long platforms in the back—careen out of control, slam into a car, and push another parked car completely onto the sidewalk and into the stairs leading to somebody's town house, right where I would have been walking had I been there sooner.

It took a moment to register that what I'd seen had really happened. I crossed to the other side of the street and passed by the scene on the nonshady side. It was worse than I'd been able to see: the truck's wheel was so bent it was almost completely off, and the front fender was crushed on the right side. A woman sat, pale, on the town house stairs, having managed to get out of her old burgundy car, now smashed like an accordion: the back was completely flat, as if there had never been a trunk, and the front looked cut off, pressed against the white car that had, until the accident, just been sitting there, parked.

Suddenly there were people standing around outside on this hot day. Three guys got out of the white truck looking dazed. The woman on the stairs said, "No, I'm all right, I'm all right," but she kept looking at her wrecked car like she couldn't make sense of it. I stood on the baking sidewalk with my sleeping daughter and looked at the debris on the ground, the previously parked car now pushed up the stairs, the glass everywhere, everyday life undone. If I had noticed my daughter was sleeping at 18th Street instead of 20th and had headed back a minute sooner, we might have been crushed by the parked car pushed onto the sidewalk, my unwieldy stroller too awkward to throw out of the way in time. If we had read books a little longer, I might have been walking up the street right there, right at that wrong time, and might have never even seen it coming.

How lucky we are, how fragile is the illusion we construct that everything is always okay, or that even if it's not, at least we're here, walking down the street safely, worrying about how to make money or meet a deadline or use up the food in the fridge before it goes bad. How foolish am I to take for granted my healthy kid who sometimes gets up countless times in the night, who likes to pretend to read *TV Guide* on the couch with me, who gets endless kicks when I substitute the word "banana" for any noun?

At the next block, I crossed back over to the other side of the street. In the distance I heard the beginnings of sirens blaring and I thought I made out the blinking of ambulance lights. Soon they'd be racing down the street, past us, to the accident.

As I headed home, I was reminded of the other accident I witnessed with my daughter. She was five months old then, still tiny; I think our cat still weighed more than she did. I had taken her to the park down by the river and was walking back home. She was in the big stroller, and I still had it in the newborn setup since she was so small: the front closed off, the back all the way down, so she could lie there staring up at the sky instead of being propped up the way an older baby would be, with her little feet too close to the unprotected edge.

She lay there, content, as we walked home. At 21st and Spruce I stopped to wait for the light. It turned green, and I was about to cross, but I looked down at my shoes for a minute, I'm not sure why. Suddenly I heard a screech, and I looked up in time to see two cars hit each other, head-on, and spin around, finally stopping six feet in front of me.

I was dazed. A woman next to me peered into my stroller

and said, "You certainly had angels watching out for *you* today." I don't usually go for the guardian angel/higher power stuff, but it hit me that she was absolutely right. My heart palpitated all the way home as I thought about what could have happened, what might have been, what I would have felt, what I might have done.

It was only after I made it safely home that I discovered I had forgotten to fasten my daughter's stroller seat belt. It hit me hard, then, how random and accidental and chancy everything is, and I held her and sobbed, imagining the unimaginable.

And then, eventually, gradually, I forgot about it.

Changed World
Mothering After September 11

The day the world forever changed for me was impossibly bright, surprisingly warm. I squinted in the pure insistence of the sunlight as cars raced by and people went on their way as if nothing momentous had happened. Everything seemed fragile and yet dangerous, incredibly vital and yet serenely dispassionate. I walked the sidewalks as if I had never walked them before, ever on the alert for something out of place, something dangerous. I was afraid. On that day I suddenly saw the world with new eyes and I was daunted by what I saw. That day was a little over two years ago, the day I brought my newborn daughter home from the hospital.

The day the world changed for nearly everyone was another impossibly bright, clear day, making what happened seem all the more incomprehensible. As the television flashed with the sickening explosion, the thoughts were: things like that don't happen on sunny days; things like that don't happen here; things like that don't happen. Later we would become commuters or New Yorkers, New Yorkers or Americans, Americans or citizens of the world; when it happened, for that horrible span of less than two hours, we were simply mourners, witnesses to the disaster. Later we would talk about what we felt or didn't feel, where we were or almost were, what we should or shouldn't do. In the moment, there was only horror. Mothers of grown sons and daughters raced to telephones to make sure their children were okay; we mothers of young children wondered how we could ever keep them safe. That day we saw the unthinkable and were haunted by it.

The events rolled like video when it all happened; months later, it comes back to me in snapshots: the unbelievable second plane; my frantic phone calls to friends in New York; billowing smoke from the Pentagon; the first tower sliding, sliding; me running to get my daughter from playschool, everyone I see on the streets talking on cell phones; later, with a friend, heading to the grocery store, overrun with people stocking up as if a hurricane were imminent; asking the woman at the checkout, "Will you get to go home early today?" and all the cashiers laughing, one of them saying, "We'll get blown up before they let us go home early." Then going home, not wanting to watch but wanting to watch; my daughter desperate to see her *Blue's Clues* video, tantruming over her fallen blocks, whining for a bottle; me forgetting to be thankful that she's alive.

It is difficult to be a mother right now, difficult to continue with the mundane when around us is the implausible. And yet I am reminded that even this difficulty—the ability to continue as we always have, to continue as we now must—is a luxury: my daughter and I are alive; we live here instead of there; this is the first time the true horror of the world has touched us. So I must continue to cut my toddler's hot dogs into quarters, slice her grapes so thin you can see through the pieces, outfit sharp corners with foam bumpers and outlets with plastic covers. I must continue my attempts to stave off the inevitable, to protect her from whatever comes next. I must continue to teach her not to hit, not to grab a toy out of a friend's or stranger's hand, not to push, not to throw; I must continue to teach her to share, to be patient, to ask politely, to say "thank you." I must continue to do this even as I try not to think about the mothers comforting their children as the planes went down, even as I try not to think about the mothers finally, cruelly knowing that they cannot save their babies from the world.

We are told that we must continue as a sign of our triumph over terror. But as mothers we must continue because our children, by virtue of their very existence, demand it. Their needs have not changed, and the immediacy of their needs has not lessened. And, amazingly, we do continue. The shock dissipates ever so slightly. Far from the epicenter of the disaster, people go on as they always have, more or less. The truck driver cuts someone off in traffic. The guy on the train talks too loudly on his cell phone. The self-absorbed friend is still the self-absorbed friend. The bills come in the mail. The same stupid commercials follow the same stupid television shows. The sun still comes up, the food still needs cooking, the diapers still need changing, the house still needs cleaning, the bills still need paying. Life, in all its inappropriateness, goes on.

"TV airplanes, Mommy," my two-year-old says after catching a brief glimpse of the omnipresent footage. "Mommy scared airplanes?" she asks after I flinch a little looking overhead at a low-flying plane. "So many flags!" she exclaims as we walk down the city streets. How can I explain to her the poignancy of her observations? How can I communicate to her the incomprehensible? How can I really talk to her about what has happened? And more important, should I?

Of course I should not. She is a toddler, barely more than a baby. Airplanes are shapes in the air, buildings are tall things she can see from our apartment. Of course she cannot know that the world has changed. I myself can barely believe it.

What she needs now is to go out in the still-potent fall sunshine and play in our neighborhood park. What she needs now is to face the day as we always have together. What she needs now is what I need: to be held, to be made to feel secure, to be soothed and hugged tight and told that everything is going to be okay. As a child, she needs desperately to hear that. And as a child, she has the luxury of being able to believe it.

The day it all happened changed the world for me, but the daily task of mothering reminds me that perhaps the world hasn't changed as much as has my perception of it. The world is still turning, terror and heartache and joy and goodness and sorrow all across its terrain, the way it always has. I am just all the more aware of it, all the more reminded to pause and be thankful for the many things I take for granted. Like the unreal certainty that the buildings I see and people I love will always be there, safe and waiting for me, and that the days will always come, one after another, unchanging.

The Concert

I hadn't been to a concert in a very long time. I used to not go because it was work: I was constantly evaluating, comparing, overlistening. Then I used to not go because it just reminded me that I am no longer performing, that I never followed the trajectory I had planned. And then I didn't go because I simply had no time. Becoming a mother has taken me worlds away from the way things used to be, and when I come across an old recital poster of mine or an old recording, it's as if I have discovered artifacts of someone else's life. You probably understand this since there are things you used to do that you no longer do. You probably understand how watching someone inhabiting your old world can give you hunger pangs.

Anyway, so I hadn't gone to a concert in a while. It's kind of ironic, since that's my day job, editing and laying out the programs for the orchestra here in town. Everyone always asks me if I get free tickets or whether I go all the time to hear them perform, and, the truth is, I never have. I've done their books for three years and I haven't gone once. But you know how it is: it's work. I can't listen to music passively; I

191

can't hear something and not think about the theory of it, the physical act of playing it. I can't help but listen critically and be snobbish about what seems to be lacking in whatever performance I'm hearing, or depressed by an incredible display of technique I know I could never personally attain. So concert-going is not a diversion for me. It's a kind of torture, listening so closely, thinking about what might have been.

But a good friend of mine, another mom, called and asked if I wanted to go to a concert the other night: a mezzo-soprano singing a program entitled "Ballad from the Feast, or, Our European Songbook of the Century." With a title like that, how could I not go, right? Against my better judgment, refined from those music-school days of accompanying torturous singers wailing through their recitals, I decided to go. A free ticket. A night out of the house, going somewhere like a real adult, without a stroller attached to my hands. What the hell.

When we arrived we mingled with the usual assortment of people who attend concerts like this: conservatory students, seasoned season-ticket holders, self-proclaimed "music lovers" (talking loudly of concerts they have been to and artists they have seen), couples on dates, many, many old people. I felt conspicuous without my baby in front of me. I felt that familiar adrenaline rush just looking at the looming concert grand onstage, and I felt both saddened and relieved that it wouldn't be me facing it.

The mezzo started in with some heavy German stuff,

straight from "Our European Songbook," I gathered. She was tiny, Japanese; she had excellent diction and she sang impressively. I scanned the bios and the program (printed up by someplace other than the magazine I work for) and saw that the singer and her accompanist were married, that they perform all over the world, together and singly, giving master classes and winning international competitions of all kinds. They were wonderful: you could tell they were married; even more, you could tell it was a good marriage, so naturally did they anticipate each other's musical choices. They never even had to look at one another. They breathed together. After a while even I had to stop listening for mistakes.

I kept asking myself, how could I have never heard of these people? I edit the bios and scan the photos of the biggest and best in the music world every day, and I'd never heard of this singer or her husband. How could they be laboring in obscurity, not registering on the public radar, when they were so good? My issue has always been perfectionism, the feeling that if I can't do something right, if I can't do it the best, if I can't do it perfectly, then I can't do it at all. So not following my musical path to its rightful, ultimate, world-dominating conclusion has left me with this hanging regret, justified in my own mind by the fact that since I couldn't ever be the best anyway, it shouldn't bother me that I'm no longer playing at the level I used to. But watching this couple perform completely blew my theory.

They didn't have big recording contracts, they didn't have big-time orchestral engagements. On paper they didn't come close to what I used to think of as the standard for musical success. But they were great, they were amazing, they were really making music. They were making people listen for an hour or two, one concert at a time.

The most powerful part, for me, was the Respighi piece called "Long Ago Times." It was the passion with which the singer sang it—plus the mention of a dead baby, which, I must admit, always makes me a little weepy now that I have a child of my own—that got me, and the sub-text, which couldn't have been more directed at me if she had sung out my name. I'll share it with you here.

> Long ago times are like
> The shadow of our dear gone life.
> A harmony now fled forever,
> A hope now faded forever,
> A sweet love without tomorrow,
> That is what long ago times are.
> How many dreams in the heart of the night
> Of that time past!
> Each day looked like a sad or happy shadow
> Which can be projected and diffused
> With the illusion that it'll last for a long time:
> This is time past!

The Concert

What biting regrets and pain
For the days so long ago!
I'm like a tiny little dead baby
Whose father is trying to wake him up,
Until all that remains
Is the memory and the regret for the days so long ago.

Zen Mom, Beginner Mom

In the beginner's mind there are many possibilities,
but in the expert's mind there are few.
—Shunryu Suzuki

We are standing in mountain pose, hands in *namaste*, our breath like the snore of a deep sleeper or the ominous exhalations of Darth Vader.

"Today, when we practice," says the yoga teacher, addressing the class, "Let's think about flexibility. The flexibility of our bodies as we breathe into the *asanas,* the flexibility of our muscles as we stretch in ways we don't get a chance to in our everyday lives. But more than that, the flexibility of our souls. Let us bring this new flexibility that we are discovering in yoga into our daily lives, so that we can approach each thing with openness and not rigidity, with seamless flow instead of resistance."

It could sound like a bunch of new-age hoo-ha if it didn't seem particularly appropriate for me. Flexibility in my daily life with a toddler would be a positive thing. I breathe through the rigorous class, stretching my hand to my ankle in triangle pose, placing the crown of my head all the way on the floor in a wide-legged forward bend. I revel in my newfound flexibility, something I never expected to celebrate when I first started classes last fall, convinced as I was then that my body would never bend in the ways it was supposed to in order to do yoga. And throughout the morning's practice, I do think about cultivating flexibility in my life, about focusing on the things I get done instead of only on the things I leave undone, about responding with enthusiasm to the detours and meanderings of a toddler's whimsy instead of feeling impatient to get on with an orderly adult routine. At the end of class, refreshed and energized, I resolve to try to maintain my inner sense of calm and face the rest of the day with a new, flexible outlook.

It lasts about ten minutes.

"I don't WANNA go home!" my daughter yells when I pick her up from her morning playschool after my class is over.

"But we have to have lunch, sweetie," I tell her.

"I don't WANNA eat lunch!" she yells back.

"Em, you need to eat a little something."

"I don't WANNA eat somefing, I wanna go to the PARK!"

Flexibility, I remind myself. "Okay, we can go to the park for a few minutes, but then we need to go home and eat lunch."

"I wanna go to the PAAAAARK!!!!" she wails as though I haven't already agreed to it.

"Em, did you hear me?" I ask through gritted teeth, my voice already taking a decidedly nonflexible tone. "I *said* we'll go to the park for a few minutes."

"I don't wanna go a few minutes, I wanna go a LOTTA minutes!" she bellows, and then collapses into hysterical tears. I stop talking and shove the stroller out the door toward the park, ignoring her tantrum while trying to remind myself to take deep yogic breaths.

Once we get to the park, my daughter refuses to get out of the stroller and stops crying only long enough to say, "I don't WANNA go to the park, I wanna go HOME and have a SWAN-ICH!"

"You want a sandwich? Fine, let's go."

Once we're home, it's more of the same. She requests a peanut butter and jelly sandwich, but when presented with a crustless sandwich, cut into triangles and nicely arranged on a plate, she dissolves into tears again. Evidently the peanut butter side of the bread cannot touch the jelly side of the bread, thereby defying the definition of a sandwich. Trying to explain this to her is useless. She tearfully demands a "peanut jelly swan-ich NOT TOUCHING, OPEN!!!!" and not in a triangle but in "big circles." Remembering how much I hated hearing the oft-uttered mom standard "This is not a restaurant!" when I was growing up, I just barely manage to hold back from shouting it myself. I go back to the drawing board, make the requested "sandwich"—two pieces of bread, one with jelly, one with peanut butter, not touching, the crusts torn off—and return only to be screamed at for having the temerity to serve it on her orange flower plate instead of her blue flower plate.

By the time I have snapped at her for freaking out over the many versions of her lunch, and she has begun a crying jag that can be resolved only by volume and sheer duration, and we have both given up on the concept of lunch and a nice afternoon together, my vision of myself as a serene yogini is thoroughly shattered.

So much for flexibility.

My husband has a book he likes to give to people as a gift. It's a collection of talks on Zen Buddhism by noted Zen master Shunryu Suzuki, called *Zen Mind, Beginner's Mind*. It's kind of a practical guidebook to Zen meditation and practice, and to Gil it sums up his general philosophy and approach to life. When he first gave me a copy of the book almost eight years ago, I read it mainly in light of my experience as a musician— all the philosophical and practical talk of practicing and spontaneity and letting go of attachment to ideas and things neatly paralleled my own teacher's talks on the philosophy and practice of making music at the piano. Now that I am a parent, I am discovering even more practical applications of this kind of Zen approach to life.

A mother needs the patience of a Zen master most days, a Zen master's wisdom and compassion and ability to remain tranquil and unmoved in the midst of chaos. Leafing through the book, reading it as a mom, several quotes jump out at me as being eerily appropriate to my decidedly untranquil life. In the section "Right Practice," I read: "The true purpose [of Zen] is to see things as they are, to observe things as they are, and to let everything go as it goes." What better advice could there be for the mother of a strong-willed toddler? Obviously, there are situations when a mother's will must supersede her child's—no, you cannot eat Skittles for dinner; no, you can't watch a video at bedtime; no, you can't put toenail polish on the cat—but for the most part, on those issues where the stakes are not so high, battling wills with a little person whose sole purpose at her age is to be oppositional will only get you both mad and exhausted. I try this kind of "right practice" from time to time, when I can remember. Emi wants to wear my old lingerie with tap shoes and a fairy crown while cutting up old junk mail with toddler scissors? Why not? Emi wants to take a bath with her bathing suit on? Fine. These are battles she can win. I can let her feel independent and autonomous as I serenely "observe things as they are, and . . . let everything go as it goes."

Another line that catches my eye: "Those who find great difficulties in practicing Zen will find more meaning in it." Substitute the words "practicing motherhood" for "practicing Zen," and perhaps you can imagine my sigh of relief and bolstered confidence upon reading that. Having difficulty in my "practice" could be a positive thing: what reassuring news!

And yet in "Right Attitude," I find: "If you lose the spirit of repetition, your practice will become quite difficult"—

which doesn't sound like the good kind of difficulty that is equated with deeper meaning. I have experienced this kind of difficulty in real life on almost a daily basis. This "spirit of repetition"—or, on a bad day, mind-numbing monotony—is a defining feature of motherhood: every day, multiple times a day, day after day, the diapers are changed, the food is prepared, the messes are cleaned, the toys are taken out, the toys are put back, the baby cries, the baby is soothed. When I find myself resenting that endless repetition, hating having to do the same tasks over and over again, facing yet again the things I thought were done that need to be redone, life is indeed difficult. Being "all Zen about it," as my husband might say, just changing the diaper or cleaning the mess or wiping the nose or cooking the food without thinking about what I'm doing or resenting that I have to keep doing it makes it easier to endure, to find a rhythm to what has to be done, to even—dare I say it?—enjoy it.

But of course, as you might expect with Zen and the art of motherhood, holding on to this sense of enjoying the repetition isn't exactly the point. Suzuki writes, "We should forget, day by day, what we have done; this is true non-attachment. And we should do something new. . . . But we should not keep holding on to anything we have done; we should only reflect on it."

Motherhood—like Zen—isn't about constant excitement, incredible self-congratulatory highs and aha moments, glimpses of enlightenment in the gleam of a well-polished countertop. According to Suzuki, "When your practice is calm and ordinary, everyday life itself is enlightenment." And it is true: I discover my most content moments as a mother when I am with my daughter, together being calm and ordinary, not struggling or resisting.

Perhaps it is just my years of practicing piano and my few months of practicing yoga that make me gravitate toward the idea, but I love the concept of the "practice" of motherhood. For one thing, approaching it as a practice implies that I don't necessarily have to be good at it right away, or even all the time; it means my mothering is a work in progress, something active, something developing. And for another, what else *is* mothering if not a constant practice? We are not born as full-fledged mothers when we birth our babies. Instead we become mothers as we live through mothering, we learn as we go, we practice our mothering as our children practice growing up, from helpless babies to tantruming toddlers to imaginative preschoolers to big kids and teens and on through adulthood. The practice of motherhood can be solitary at times, but it can also be done in concert with others; it can feel unproductive some days and exhilarating on others. Mothering is something you can understand only while you're doing it. And the minute you think you really get it, your moment of enlightenment is shattered—what worked to soothe your child yesterday no longer works today, the routine you thought you had mastered is rendered obsolete as your baby finally abandons a morning nap or begins to walk. Mothering is a koan, and the only definitive answer is that there is no answer, only the puzzling out of an answer. The practice is constant, and it is never-ending, as our children grow and change and move from stage to stage, presenting us with new issues to tackle, new riddles to ponder. Like music, like Zen, like yoga, in mothering the motto is not "practice makes perfect" but perhaps simply "practice makes practice." There is no ending point, just a multitude of points along the way.

Real life is not as neat and philosophical as it is in my husband's favorite book or in my yoga class. There are some days I can be the kind of Zen mom I'd ideally love to be all the time. And there are others—and I admit there are more of these kinds of days than the former—where I am exasperated and resentful and irritated and overwhelmed and decidedly un-Zen and inflexible in my mothering. But the point, I suppose, is to try to be aware of the difference. So I try to practice mothering as best I can. I try to apply the openness of the Zen "beginner's mind" and the willingness to be flexible that I cultivate in yoga to my daily life with my daughter. I'm not always successful in these attempts, but at the very least I am succeeding in making them.

Back in yoga class, I try to focus on my breath, on being centered, on reveling in this opportunity to recharge myself and emerge with a renewed, refreshed perspective. Today in class the teacher talks about the intrinsic value of everything, the truth that nearly everything we experience and encounter has some meaning we can learn from, and she relates one of my favorite Zen stories. A few thousand years ago, someone asked the Zen master Un Mun, "What is Buddha nature?" and he gave his disciples the shocking and surprising answer, "Dry shit on a stick." My answer as a mom might have been "Dry shit on a diaper," but I understand what he was talking about.

Piano Lessons

My daughter has always been my harshest musical critic. Even when she was just a few months old, she had clearly defined opinions about my playing. I remember placing her in her Super-Saucer when she was about five months old, and dragging it close to our baby grand, preparing us for a musical salon, a domestic tableau worthy of *Martha Stewart Baby* magazine. I had envisioned the scene playing out with me providing my eagerly receptive daughter with live performances of brain-enriching Mozart, mathematics-improving Bach, and atmospheric, brooding Chopin. The reality of it was that as soon as I turned toward the piano and began my perform-ance, Emi started screaming. And she wouldn't stop screaming until I stopped playing. Everyone's a critic.

As Emi grew older, I kept trying to see whether the sce-nario would change. Thinking perhaps it was my choice of repertoire she disapproved of, I tried in vain to find some-thing that pleased her refined musical sensibilities, but she rejected it all: Beethoven, Mozart, Chopin, Prokofiev, Bach, Rachmaninoff, even Brahms. Even the pieces I had practiced over and over with her inside me failed to soothe. I remember working on Beethoven's Appassionata piano sonata when I was pregnant, loving how whenever I'd get to a dramatic part she would kick and kick inside me. At the time I assumed all that activity meant she was enjoying the music. Now I was being forced to consider that perhaps even in utero she was telling me to stop.

Sometimes I'd try to talk to her about it, even when she was far too young understand or to talk back. "Come on," I'd say. "Haven't you read the studies? Mozart is *good* for babies. Babies *like* it." Or, more exasperated: "You know, most babies would be thrilled to have their very own *Baby Mozart* sound track at home! Most kids would love it if their mommies could play real music for them! What's your problem?" Or, finally at my wit's end: "This is what I used to *do*! This was my life before you were here! Don't you care???" Eventually, desperate to have some contact with the keyboard (and by extension, with my old life) and to instill in her some measure of musical appreciation, I capitulated to her demands and stopped trying to play my old classical repertoire, instead plying her with songs she might recognize. "How about 'Elmo's World'? 'Twinkle, Twinkle'?" I'd ask her, staring at her little chubby cheeks, her wide eyes watching me warily. But unless she was sitting on my lap, slapping the keys with her pudgy hands and making sure my fingers were nowhere near the keyboard, the result was always the same.

At some point I gave up trying to impress her with my musical abilities. I still encouraged her to explore our piano, which was increasingly becoming a piece of furniture rather than a musical instrument, as I no longer had the time (or her permission) to play, but I stopped trying to force an appreciation of Mommy's non-Emi-related skills. When she was eighteen months old, she did allow me to show her the difference between low notes and high notes, and by the time she was two, she thought it was fun to play the piano "like a little tiny bug" or "like a big fat cat," but I had backed off in my attempts at a formal introduction to music. At least I was reassured by that point that her severe musical criticism was not only reserved for my playing: if my husband even so much as hummed idly under his breath, she'd command, "Stop singing!" And if we were driving in the car and happened to turn on the radio, she'd yell, "No music! Just news!"

I'm told by my parents that I first saw a real piano when I was two. After having my hands wiped clean and being instructed to press only one key at a time, I was allowed to try it. As the story goes, I played one note and then another, and then I looked up at my mother. "Mom," I told her, "I *have* to play the piano!" My parents, though, were discouraged from signing me up for early piano lessons, the theory being that any child under eight years old was simply too young for any kind of formal training. So I was made to wait.

I finally received piano lessons as a gift for my eighth

birthday. I may have gotten other presents that year, but if I did, I don't remember them. What I remember is my first lesson: how tall and imposing the piano teacher seemed, how her house smelled, how the music room where she taught was dark and piled with sheet music and sticker books, how her piano keyboard seemed wider than I was tall, how even if I stretched out my arms I couldn't seem to reach both extremes of bass and treble. I even remember the first song she taught me. She showed me middle C, explained to me about finger numbers (big thumbs on both hands being one, indexes two, middle fingers three, ring fingers four, and pinkies five) and opened a music book filled with cartoons and giant bubbles of music notes. My first assignment: a little fifteen-note ditty called "At the Fair," an introduction to the notes middle-C, D and E. She showed it to me, demonstrating how to plunk it out with the correct fingers, and before she was through playing it twice, I had it. Triumphant, I played that song over and over, for anyone who would listen. If I wasn't near a piano, I'd sing it for people. I remember my father's bemused expression when I performed my incredible accomplishment for him. He seemed both proud and amused that anyone could be so excited over such an inane series of notes.

My six years of waiting were finally over: I was finally able to play the piano. The only snag in that plan was the simple fact that we didn't have one. For six months I practiced on pianos at friends' houses, on the out-of-tune clunker in the school cafeteria, on the keyboardless smoothness of our kitchen table. Finally, when I showed up at one of my lessons surprising my teacher by having taught myself Beethoven's "Für Elise" (oh, how painstakingly I counted out each line and space, decoding the names of the notes, trying to interpret all the squiggles of rests and shooting planes of crescendos!), she consulted with my parents and urged them to find a piano—any piano—for me to have at home. That first piano, a little sixty-eight-key spinet, didn't last long. By the time I'd been playing a year, I was working on repertoire that needed more keys (a normal keyboard has eighty-eight), and the piano itself was literally wearing out through the sheer force of my practice. After being called to our house for, as he put it, the "umpteenth time" to fix a key stubbornly stuck in its keybed, refusing to be struck any longer in the service of my music making, our piano tuner (Mr. Swackhammer, a wonderful piano-tuner name) exasperatedly pleaded with my parents, "Please! Get this kid a real piano!"

To their credit, they did. We trolled the piano stores, looking for a likely candidate. It had to fulfill two qualifications: it had to fit in our house, and it had to be cheap. Luckily we found one that was both. Our Everett grand, with real ivory keys, sat in our tiny house, surrounded by three cats, a dog, three kids, and various guests after its previous sedate life as living room furniture for a little old lady. I loved it. It was so massive, and so loud. Everything

I played seemed more dramatic, more powerful, and if I ever played with the lid open, it was booming enough that the whole neighborhood could hear.

When we made the move to Southern California, after I'd been playing piano for about a year and a half, our piano did not appreciate it. The insult of being dismantled and trucked from Humboldt County to San Diego did not sit well with it, and by the time it was correctly reassembled and set up in our new place, the heat and humidity of the move had permanently marked its demise. Ivories began popping off; it stopped holding its tune. But still I kept playing. Both my sisters were learning the piano by that point as well, so there were three of us competing for practice time. We realized the impact of our ivory-less keyboard when it was discovered that my youngest sister couldn't play her pieces on other, intact pianos because she had been using our piano's pockmarked landscape for visual landmarks: middle-C was the one without an ivory sheath on it, low G had an ivory on it but the A and F on either side did not. Eventually this problem was solved by our piano, which continued to shed its ivories to the point where we were just playing on the naked wood of the keys.

By the time I had been playing for two years, I started participating in local piano competitions. My usual competitors were kids who had been playing since before they could walk, their parents evidently either not receiving or completely ignoring the advice my parents had so carefully followed concerning the proper timing of music lessons. But it didn't seem to matter: for all my lack of training and experience, I was winning. As I progressed through junior high and then high school, the competition season became more and more of a formality, with the same familiar faces taking home trophies and prizes, the same judges evaluating us year after year. There were five or six of us out of the usual competition-circuit crowd who would take turns winning, and consequently it wasn't as much about beating someone as it was about having a turn at the top of the podium. Competing every other weekend during the busy season wasn't as taxing as it might sound: it was a chance to perform and be critiqued, and after years of doing it, performing wasn't the nerve-wracking experience you might think it would be. It felt natural to be playing onstage, and the rush of adrenaline wasn't because I was afraid of making a mistake but rather due to the sheer exhilaration of making music and playing well.

Later, when I embarked on my conservatory training, the fear would set in. Suddenly going into the cocoon of serious study, with the point being to hibernate in the practice rooms and work diligently in solitude, emerging at the end of my stint there a fully formed musical butterfly, took me off the track of constant performance. I still somewhat enjoyed performing, when I did it, but I discovered that after so much time listening to my playing bouncing off the soundproofed walls of a practice room, the recital stage was quite daunting.

I no longer thrived on the stressful thrill of performance and perfection, finding it instead merely stressful, and thrilling only when the performance was finally over. Still, I realized that the ease of performance that seemed so natural in my younger days was mostly because I didn't know as much about what I was doing. I knew it was simply a matter of time, and balance and hard work, before I would be able to combine the joy of knowledgeless playing with informed music-making.

That is always the question, with the piano: balance. Balance between the left hand and the right hand, balance between the melody and the harmony, balance between soft and loud, balance between showmanship and musicianship, balance between interpretation and technique. It is the manner of integration that is the answer, that defines a player's talent, that makes someone a piano player or an artist.

As a mother I am also constantly addressing the question of balance, trying to weigh my own wants and needs against my daughter's, trying to balance my interests with hers. Sometimes that can be difficult to sort out. Do I want her to develop a love of music and books because those are things that are good for a kid to appreciate, or do I want her to be interested in them to justify my own interest in them, thereby bringing us closer together, enmeshing us a little more than we already are? Did I want her to want to play piano at age two because I didn't get to, to love it so as to justify my own unrequited love for it? Do I let her choose a video to watch because she no longer naps and needs some downtime, or because I desperately want to sit on the couch and read something in a book that does not contain the words "cat in the hat"? Where do her best interests begin and mine end?

Shortly after her third birthday, Emi and I lounged on a lazy afternoon watching that turtle cartoon, *Franklin*. In that particular episode, Franklin wanted to learn how to play the piano, but he didn't want to actually practice. After observing his friends diligently practicing away for the big piano recital, though, he realized that he couldn't expect to just spontaneously develop an ability to play, and he got down to the work of practicing. Emi was rapt, glued to the TV, hanging on every twist and turn of the fifteen-minute plot. Watching Franklin go home and sit at his piano, trying to figure out how to play a song by ear, she suddenly recognized the tune he was plunking out. "Mommy!" she exclaimed. "That's 'Twinkle, Twinkle, Little Star'!" She was absolutely right, that was indeed what Franklin was trying to play. Emi has always been good at recognizing music: I still remember her surprising holiday shoppers in the local department store when she was two by pointing out that the Muzak over the sound system was "Nutcracker music." (I guess all those wintry afternoons of watching her ballet video of Tchaikovsky's "The Nutcracker" on endless repeat paid off.)

"That's right," I told her. "Franklin's learning how to play 'Twinkle, Twinkle.'"

"Yeah!" she said, not looking away from the screen. We watched the rest of the episode, witnessing Franklin's friends and Franklin himself perform their piano songs in their class at school. When it was done, she told me excitedly, "Mommy, Franklin played 'Twinkle, Twinkle' all by himself on the piano! He did it!" And I thought, well, it's been a while, why not try again. So I asked as nonchalantly as I possibly could, "Hey, would *you* like to play the piano? Just like Franklin?" To my surprise, her answer this time was a very excited, emphatic "YES."

We sat at the piano, side by side. I was still trying to play it cool and act as though I couldn't care less whether or not Emi really wanted to play or whether she just wanted to play around.

"Would you like me to show you a song?" I asked, expecting the usual answer to that question, which is "NO!" Instead, she surprised me.

"Yeah, Mommy! Show me a song!"

I racked my brain back to my days of teaching young kids. What little song could I show her that she could easily master, thereby giving her a taste of accomplishment and whetting her appetite to come back for more piano another time? But she already had something in mind.

"I want to play 'Twinkle, Twinkle,' just like Franklin!" she exclaimed excitedly.

Despite its popularity at circle times and toddler music classes across the country, "Twinkle, Twinkle" is actually a pretty difficult song to start out with, what with the big leap at the beginning that can disorient young players who aren't yet familiar with the piano landscape, and the ideal though not always practical demand of using every single finger of the hand to play it. Still, if "Twinkle, Twinkle" was what it was going to take to capture her interest, then "Twinkle, Twinkle" it was going to be.

First I played it for her myself, both of us singing along. Then I opted for the one-finger method of plunking it out, taking her index finger and placing it on each note as we sang the familiar lyrics. We did that twice, maybe three times, and then she said, "Let ME do it! I do it all my by-self!" And, believe it or not, she did. I showed her where to start and pointed to the note she needed to jump to when it came time for the big leap, but she did it. All my by-self.

As soon as she finished, she gasped with excitement. "Mommy, I did it!" she exclaimed. "I did 'Twinkle, Twinkle' all my by-self!" And she hugged me so tight, I wasn't sure whether it was her enthusiastic grip or my maternal pride that was making my eyes prick with tears. This is ridiculous, I thought to myself. I'm tearing up like one of those sports moms, like one of those stage moms, like one of those . . . moms! I tried not to make my reaction out of proportion to hers, so as not to weight the moment with any more importance than it already held, but I couldn't help my insane rush of pride: my baby had done it, she had played her first piece of music.

She played it over and over, getting better each time, and each time ending with the excited cry of, "I did it! Let's do it again!" and squeezing me with a hug. She was so excited, so proud of herself, so elated by her accomplishment. It reminded me of my eight-year-old self, stringing together notes and for the first time really making the profound connection that keys pressed in a certain order in a certain rhythm makes melody makes music. Watching my own daughter make that thrilling connection, watching her as she scrambled to "play my song for Daddy" when he came home, watching her face explode in a beatific smile as she finished each time, brought me back to the place where I started. That ultimate, perfect joy, unclouded by expectation or critique or any question of balance.

Mother Land

The early years of motherhood are all about reconciling your pre-kid ideals with the reality of life as a mother. Some women fight this assimilation kicking and screaming; others accept the all-consuming life of a mom as inevitable. For most of us, it is a gradual process. Before the baby's born we're planning our homemade organic baby meals. Six months later we're desperately trying to shovel in at least one spoonful ("Please! before you starve!") of rice cereal we mixed from a box. Two years after that we're overjoyed to discover our toddler likes Pop-Tarts, because at least they're packed with vitamins.

It's like this with pretty much everything. Our staunch ideals of how we will raise our children get significantly reshaped by those very kids once they're here in the world running us ragged, wearing down our defenses, leaving us no choice but to embark on that slippery slope and say, "Just this once!" to stop the whining. It's true, some of my friends have managed to cling to a few of their firm beliefs—I have one friend who's successfully brainwashed her kid into thinking he doesn't like chocolate, and another whose kid hasn't ever watched TV—but for the most part, my peers, like me, have embarked on the eternal compromise that is dealing with a toddler. We are no longer inexperienced, we are no longer naively confident that our superb parenting skills will produce the perfectly well-behaved mini-adult, we are willing to admit that for the most part we simply want to get through the day. We have been broken in. So we pick our battles.

This sounds pretty normal, unless you're new to the mom game, in which case you probably can't imagine your pudgy, dimpled newborn telling you, "Go away RIGHT NOW, MOMMY!" or turning into a two-year-old drama queen or refusing to wear anything but a hideously pink Princess Barbie outfit with red tights and cowboy boots—or doing anything other than gaze at you lovingly and coo. The gap between new moms and broken-in moms is almost as unfathomable as the gap between pregnant women and new mothers: you just don't fully get it until you're there.

So how do you know you're there? How do you know you've finally crossed over into Mother land? It's not as though after your kid's first tantrum in a public place the Prize Patrol will show up with a wreath and a check congratulating you for graduating to the ranks of the broken-in. Most likely you won't even realize it's happened until some incident makes it clear that you are no longer the parent you thought you were.

For me, it was a birthday party. A friend's baby had reached that major milestone of turning one, and my then two-year-old and I were invited to the party. It was a packed affair, wall-to-wall one-year-olds and newborns with tired moms looking their best in party clothes and spit-up-stained slings. My daughter wasn't interested in any of the healthful baby hors d'oeuvres the gracious hostess had provided, but she was able to cadge some Goldfish crackers from the kitchen. She wandered around, checking out the birthday boy's haul while she grazed on Goldfish out of a Pixie cup. At some point, more interested in a balloon than in her cup of fish, she dropped the cup, spilling bright-orange crackers all over the floor. I swooped in to clean up the mess before anyone stepped on the Goldfish, scooped them all back into the cup, and gave the cup back to my daughter, who promptly dug in and crammed a few of the fallen fish into her mouth.

I looked up just in time to catch a glimpse of a new mom witnessing the proceedings in absolute terror. In her gaping mouth, emitting a silent scream of horror, and her white-knuckled hands protectively gripping her squirming newborn, I saw a version of myself before I had been broken in. It was the look of a woman who knew above all that A) her child would never consume artificially orange crackers loaded with partially hydrogenated soybean oil, but B) if by some freak event such ingestion did occur, it would certainly *not* take place after said crackers had been picked up *off the floor*!

It was then that I realized I'd made it: I had officially

graduated to the ranks of the broken-in mom. I didn't care that my kid was eating Goldfish crackers off someone else's floor—my God, she was *eating*! That was good enough for me. In fact, I hadn't even given it a second thought until I saw the other mom's reaction. True, there was an awkward silence as I stood up, brushing my hands of Goldfish crumbs and wondering what to say, but luckily the new baby started fussing and my daughter started shoving some poor kid, so we both had our duties to attend to.

I remember being eighteen and visiting my aunt, who had just had her second baby. We were driving to a park to let the older child, who was almost two, let off some steam. On the way there, the kid gnawed on a graham cracker for a while, and when we got to the park, he handed it off to his mom, who automatically popped it in her mouth and ate it. Being eighteen, I was, of course, completely revolted. My aunt looked at me.

"What?" she said, amused. "You think that's gross?"

"Well, yeah," I said. "It was totally covered with drool."

She laughed and looked at me and sighed. "Believe me, drool is the least of it, my dear. At this point, drool is *nothing*!"

At the time I thought, well, there it is. That's how you know you're ready to be a mom: you don't care about drooly graham crackers and other disgusting things.

Now of course I realize there is not a moment when you suddenly master your revulsion of saliva and embrace motherhood; now of course I realize that a soggy, chewed-on graham cracker often represents a meal for a sleep-deprived mom on the go. Now of course I realize I have crossed many a breaking-in point since that afternoon twelve years ago, from being grossed out by a little cousin's drool to being terrified of giving birth to being haunted by the fear of being a bad mom to being resigned to the fact that I have a two-year-old ballet- and princess-loving Cinderella fan who's still hooked on the bottle. At each point along the way— enduring an epidural-free birth, finding comfort in writing about my experience of motherhood, humbly surviving the first year and beyond and accepting my daughter's inimitable personality and her experience of the world—I have had to put aside my preconceptions, my ego, my attachment to how I think things should be. And even though some days I wince at what the pre-kid me would think about letting my daughter watch *The Wiggles* for the third time in a row, for the most part I'm glad to be a little less rigid, a little softer, broken in like my favorite jeans.

Now, if you moms of teenagers could kindly stop laughing at me . . .

After Shock

I end this book the way it began: with a pregnancy.

Yes, with all my doubt, with all my fear, with all my misgivings about being cut out for the work of a mother, I am making the descent again—descending into my body, into the womb of the first housebound weeks and months of newborn life, into the beginning again. It wasn't as much a conscious decision as it was poor planning, but I'm under no illusions this time that it could have happened any other way.

There are a lot of differences this time. This time I am not my own person, I am already a mother. I have no time to savor the novelty of carrying a life within me, no time to read up on what to expect each week, no time to keep a diary of my progress. This time I have only the persistent hopes that my toddler will become a born-again napper, that I'll get through the day without puking in public, that I'll persevere through to the part where I feel like a normal person again—or as normal a person as you can be when your belly is bulging with some sort of World Cup soccer tournament going on inside and it is only a matter of weeks before that invisible unceasing kicker is painfully revealed as a helpless, squalling newborn human being.

This time I do not have the same questions. This time I am not asking how will I love as a mother, how will I be as a mother, what will it be like to be a mother, but rather: what will it be like to be a mother of two? how will I stretch my energy, stretch my love around two little beings with such different needs? This time the learning curve will be different, not the nervous new-parent questions of whether the baby will stop breathing, whether I could break her by holding her the wrong way. The skill level is increasing but the basics are the same. Last time I was learning how to juggle; this time I am throwing a few more fiery clubs into the air.

This time I know what to expect without thumbing through reference books, but more important I know that even what I expect may not happen. I know I do not have the control I thought was mine the first time around, and consequently this time the weeks fly by, the months progress without my constant vigilance, and I can do the real work of preparing for what does not come naturally for me: postpartum recovery.

My goal with this pregnancy has been to take the element of surprise out of everything I possibly can, in hopes of being better prepared for what comes next. Last time, even with all my hyper-preparedness, surprise was the overriding theme of my whole experience. Surprise, the epidural isn't working! Surprise, breast-feeding isn't working either! Surprise, I can't work from home with a newborn! Surprise, this is not going as I had planned! Surprise, I don't love being a mom! This time I am planning for being constantly buffeted by the surprises of perplexity and disappointment. This time I am planning to expect the unexpected, planning for all the possibilities, not only the ones I'd like to see happen. I am planning away the element of surprise in the hopes that I'll actually be surprised at how different, how possibly much better, the second time around can be.

Writing much of this book about being a new mother of one child while preparing for baby number two has cast my first experience of motherhood in an entirely new light. Revisiting those difficult first postpartum months, I find myself comparing that period to my current hectic life with a strong-willed toddler and wondering, "Was life with a newborn really so bad? She couldn't move, couldn't talk, couldn't yell at me. How was that so difficult?" And it's true that there are days when those bleak moments of maternal doubt and insecurity and sleep deprivation do seem like pleasant alternatives to the meltdowns and tantrums of the terrible twos and threes. But I know that it really *was* that difficult back then, that just because parenting now presents new challenges and difficulties doesn't mean its earlier trials were negligible.

What I know this time that I didn't before is that everything could have happened differently, and in some ways my fears are darker this time, as I realize now what might have been but was not. What if my labor and delivery is more complicated this time? What if this next child is not healthy? What if this next baby isn't as lucky? I know now to be thankful for the luxury of my troubles, the luxury of a relatively ordinary life, with no more than the usual financial worries, the usual random diaper rash. We made it two years without an ear infection, nearly three and a half years without any major medical emergencies. It could have all been different, and I am not only incredibly thankful that it was not, but also humbled enough to accept that this time, with this new baby, things may not go as smoothly.

This time I know that I am emotionally serene while I am pregnant, emotionally turbulent postpartum. Pregnant, I am floating in still water. Postpartum I tumble down a waterfall and into the raging rapids.

Last time each kick was Morse code meant for only me to decipher. This time each kick is a reminder that there is an actual human baby inside me, and that at some point that baby is going to have to come out. Each squirm, each movement, reminds me that this period of stability will soon be ending, and I will be thrust back to the beginning.

Last time I was pregnant in the chill of winter, my ever-expanding belly draped in sweaters, heavy coats, protected from the elements. This time I am pregnant in the stifling heat of summer, my body stretched to its limit in as little clothing as possible, for all passersby to see.

Last time I was pregnant with a girl. This time I am pregnant with a boy.

Last time I made the passage through mother shock, coming out clear on the other side, and now I am one of those women who can freely converse about hemorrhoids, stitches, labor, pain. Now I am one of those women with Pull-Ups and extra Snow White panties in her purse. Now I am one of those women who can tell you how many diapers are left in the bag and where Mr. Potato Head's left arm is. Now I am one of those women who can change a dirty diaper standing up while eating lunch without losing my appetite. Now I am one of those women I saw in the park, back when I was a new mother, one of those women fully at home in their motherhood, able to shape-shift from Mommy to human being without the discombobulating shock of suddenly being no longer one or the other. And now that I am well on my way to being a mother of two—and well on my way to finally facing my fear of the double stroller—my motherhood is cemented. There is no question, no doubt, no avoiding it: I am officially, really, fully a mother.

This time, when I make the crossing into motherhood the second time around, I know my body is the map, my mind is the guidebook, my heart is the compass. This time I know that despite my best attempts, no amount of preparedness can truly prepare me for what may come.

Will I have the same postpartum fears I had last time? Will I still wonder whether or not I am capable of handling the work of being a mother? Will I still have days when I wish I could run away, hop a bus, and be gone from my crazy, overwhelming life? I imagine that I probably will, that I will most likely still think and worry and be concerned about these things—but this time I won't have as much free time to dwell on them.

This time I have all the necessary equipment—the slings and bouncy seats of outrageous fortune—and this time I am bolstered by having had the necessary experience. This time I am as ready as I can ever be, humbled and nervous and eager to meet my new tour guide in this next journey through mother land.

Notes and Credits

Mother Love

Kalervo Oberg quotes in all sections are from *Culture Shock: Psychological Reactions to Unfamiliar Environments* by Adrian Furnham and Stephen Bochner. New York, NY: Methuen & Co., 1986. Copyright © 1986 by Kalervo Oberg.

Quote from the University of Iowa Web site on culture shock is from http://www.uiowa.edu/~uiabroad/predeparture/PREPAREculture_shock.html

Nora Okja Keller quote is from "You'll Get Used to It" by Nora Okja Keller. From *Mothers Who Think* edited by Camille Peri and Kate Moses. New York, NY: Washington Square Press, 1999. Copyright © 1999 by *Salon Magazine*.

Madeleine L'Engle quote is from *Celebrating Mothers: A Book of Appreciation* edited by Glorya Hale and Carol Kelly-Gangi. New York, NY: MetroBooks, 2002. Copyright © 2002 by MetroBooks.

Mother Shock

Quote from Whitman College's Web site on culture shock

is from http://www.whitman.edu/offices_departments/study_abroad/cultureshock.htm

Jane Lazarre quote is from *The Mother Knot* by Jane Lazarre. Durham, NC: Duke University Press, 1997. Copyright © 1997 by Duke University Press. Used by permission of the publisher.

Adrienne Rich quote is from "Anger and Tenderness" by Adrienne Rich. From *Of Woman Born: Motherhood as Experience and Institution* by Adrienne Rich. New York, NY: W.W. Norton & Company, 1986. Copyright © 1976, 1986 by W. W. Norton & Company, Inc.

Doris Lessing quote is from *Under My Skin: Volume One of My Autobiography to 1949* by Doris Lessing. New York, NY: HarperCollins Publishers, 1994. Copyright © 1994 by Doris Lessing.

Mother Tongue
Quote from the University of Iowa Web site on culture shock is from http://www.uiowa.edu/~uiabroad/predeparture/PREPAREculture_shock.html

Susan Griffin quote is from "Feminism and Motherhood" by Susan Griffin. From *Made from This Earth: An Anthology of Writings* by Susan Griffin. London: Women's Press Ltd., 1982. Copyright © 1982 by Susan Griffin.

Sara Ruddick quote is from "Talking about 'Mothers'" by Sara Ruddick. From *Maternal Thinking: Toward a Politics of Peace* by Sara Ruddick. Boston, MA: Beacon Press, 1999. Copyright © 1989 by Sara Ruddick.

"Advice You Can Bank On: Straighten Up Your Room-A Study Finds That Kids Who Live in Tidy Homes Are Likely to Clean Up Financially" is from the *Washington Post*, April 3, 2001; Page T6; Health Section

Mother Land

Quote from the University of Iowa Web site on culture shock is from http://www.uiowa.edu/~uiabroad/predeparture/ PREPAREculture_shock.html

Susan Cheever quote is from *As Good As I Can Be* by Susan Cheever. New York, NY: Simon & Schuster, 2002. Copyright © 2002 by Susan Cheever. Used by permission of the publisher.

Joy Harjo quote is from *Celebrating Mothers: A Book of Appreciation* edited by Glorya Hale and Carol Kelly-Gangi. New York, NY: MetroBooks, 2002. Copyright © 2002 by Joy Harjo.

Marni Jackson quote is from *The Mother Zone* by Marni Jackson. Toronto: MacFarlane, Walter & Ross, 1992. Copyright © 1992 by Marni Jackson.

Acknowledgments

Many thanks:

To my wonderful agent, Laura Gross, who was enthusiastic and excited about this project back when it existed only as a nice idea for a book title, and to Madeline Simon, my thoughtful and talented friend who introduced us.

To Maureen Welsh, for the loan of her laptop computer, and the good people at Tuscany Café, who kept me well stocked with lemon-poppy muffins and diet Cokes while I occupied my usual table with said laptop, writing this book and hogging the only electrical outlet in the joint.

To the founding members of Baby Club, Elise Luce Kraemer, Karen Klein, and Shawna Goodman, who saved my sanity on a daily basis that first year . . . and to the members of my online mothers' group—Shannon, Andrea, Michelle, Katie, Lisa, Gretchen, Minna, Kristen, Shell, Karen, Jennifer, Diane, Heather, and Anne—who over the past three years have been so supportive.

To Elizabeth LaBan for reading and critiquing many first drafts of many of these essays, and for always being honest in her responses.

To my family and friends for listening to me ramble incessantly about motherhood and this book (especially Angie Goldberg, who is now a mother herself).

To all of Emi's grandparents, Bill and Elin Buchanan and Steve and Nurit Binenbaum, whom I especially thank for the free baby sitting in addition to their general support.

To Gil, for his encouragement, feedback, and patience, and for his self-admittedly pathetic yet very much appreciated attempts at keeping Emi occupied so I could write.

And finally to Emi, who sparked my transformation from regular person to mother, and from writing mother to published author, providing at all times along the way an endless source of love, joy, and, of course, material.

ANDREA BUCHANAN is a writer whose work has been featured in the collection *Breeder: Real-Life Stories from the New Generation of Mothers* and in various online parenting magazines, including her Web site for Philadelphia-area mothers, PhillyMama.com. Before she was a mother, she was a classical pianist. Her last recital was at Carnegie Hall, back before she knew how to play the Teletubbies theme song. Andrea lives with her family in Philadelphia.

Selected Live Girls Titles from Seal Press

The Big Rumpus: A Mother's Tales from the Trenches by Ayun Halliday. $15.95, 1-58005-071-9.

Growing Seasons: Half-baked Garden Tips, Cheap Advice about Marriage and Questionable Theories on Motherhood by Annie Spiegelman. $14.95, 1-58005-079-4.

The Mother Trip: Hip Mama's Guide to Staying Sane in the Chaos of Motherhood by Ariel Gore. $14.95, 1-58005-029-8.

Breeder: Real-Life Stories from the New Generation of Mothers edited by Ariel Gore and Bee Lavender. $16.00, 1-58005-051-4.

The Moment of Truth: Women's Funniest Romantic Catastrophes edited by Kristin Beck. $14.95, 1-58005-069-7.

Chelsea Whistle by Michelle Tea. $14.95, 1-58005-073-5.

Young Wives' Tales: New Adventures in Love and Partnership edited by Jill Corral and Lisa Miya-Jervis, foreword by bell hooks. $16.95, 1-58005-050-6. Wife.

Bare Your Soul: The Thinking Girl's Guide to Enlightenment edited by Angela Watrous. $16.95, 1-58005-076-X.

Seal Press publishes many books of fiction and nonfiction by women writers. Please visit our Web site at www.sealpress.com.